Cases in

Marketing Management

DALE L. VARBLE
Western Michigan University

CHARLES E. MERRILL PUBLISHING COMPANY
A Bell & Howell Company
Columbus, Ohio

To Mary Ellen

Published by
CHARLES E. MERRILL PUBLISHING COMPANY
A Bell & Howell Company
Columbus, OH 43216

This book was set in Helvetica.
The production editors were Susan Glick and Laura Harder.
The cover was designed by Will Chenoweth.

International Standard Book Number: 0-675-08638-8
Library of Congress Catalog Card Number: 75-26476

1 2 3 4 5 6 7 8 — 82 81 80 79 78 77 76

Printed in the United States of America

PREFACE

This book is a marketing casebook. It is to encourage and teach students to learn and apply the marketing principles and concepts. In order to accomplish this, several factors have been considered in compiling the book. The forty-six cases were selected to stress reality. Most of the cases are not discrete, single-issue oriented, although one issue can easily be selected and emphasized by the instructor, if desired. Formulation of the problem or decisions to be made is intended to be a challenge as it normally is in real-life situations. Thus, relevant and irrelevant information and facts are given. The student is expected to develop the ability to separate the important from the unimportant. The cases also revolve around people. People with aspirations, prejudices, enthusiasm and various other weaknesses and strengths — real people.

Cases were selected to stress various marketing activities and institutions. Each section is based on a major marketing activity and within each section secondary marketing activities and concepts are stressed. Various types of marketing institutions are represented in the case material.

The cases also vary in length and complexity. The shorter cases can be equally as difficult as the longer cases but typically are more abstract, thus allowing the student to make more assumptions and in this respect be more creative. The longer cases challenge the student in terms of analyzing and keeping facts straight.

The book is designed to be used in conjunction with a textbook or readings book. It also works well as a supplement for instructors who have freed themselves from textbooks and use their own specially prepared materials. Several features were included to make it especially easy to use as a supplement. The first chapter, "Use of the Case Method" introduces the student to case analysis. It includes explanations of the learning value of the use of cases, an outline of the scientific method and illustrative case and student analysis. Typically these explanations are left to the instructor and can be easily overlooked. The cases are divided into topic areas commonly used in marketing. The manual relates each case to specific chapters of popular marketing texts. A discussion of the art of making presentations, both oral and written, and an appendix, which can be used at any time, also makes the book a good supplement. It might also be noted that the cases are basically at the undergraduate level in difficulty.

Much of the material has been used in one form or another in my marketing courses at Western Michigan University. The form of the cases and the cases used has resulted, to a great extent, from the reactions of my students. Much credit goes to them for their contributions and patience.

For providing invaluable editorial assistance and many fresh ideas, I'm most appreciative to Dr. David C. Sleeper, University of South Florida; Dr. L. J. Konopa, Kent State University; and Dr. Thomas Webb, Dalton, Dalton, Little and Newport. I am grateful to Dr. Reginald A. Graham, Fort Lewis College; Dr. Hugh Law, East Tennessee State University; Dr. Kung-Mo Kuo, The University of Wisconsin-Platteville; Mr. William Frances, Gerber Products, and many, many other companies and individuals for contributing cases. Unfortunately not all of the cases contributed could be used because of space limitations.

At Western Michigan University, Darrell Jones, Dean of the College of Business, and Robert Trader, Chairman of the Marketing Department, have provided an atmosphere conducive to intellectual achievement and specific administrative assistance in the completion of this casebook. Finally I'm thankful to Mary Ellen, my wife, who, through her patience, motivation, and many other contributions, has made this book possible.

To all of these people, plus many others too numerous to mention, I am most grateful. The book would not have been possible without their assistance. I, however, am responsible for all errors and omissions.

Dale L. Varble

Kalamazoo, Michigan

CONTENTS

chapter

1

Use of the
Case Method

A marketing case is a description of a marketing situation, any situation which directly affects the development and/or exchange of goods and services. This description is made from a point of view: from an omnipotent view, from that of employees, or from that of an individual outside the organization. Consequently, the accuracy, relevance, and completeness of the information presented in a case should not be automatically assumed, since it does reflect a view point.

As might be expected, the description may take many forms: outline word description, statistical data, narrative description — all are possible. Similarly, the context may vary: a description of an existing situation, a historical one, or a completely imaginary one.

The Case Method:
A Learning Device

The case is an excellent vehicle for learning concepts and practicing application of those concepts. The learning environment created by using cases has some very special characteristics. A case problem demands the learning of basic principles and concepts if a solution to the problem is to be found. When the concepts are known, the case approach presents the opportunity to become involved and apply the knowledge to a specific situation. Applying knowledge can be more difficult than learning basic concepts. The risk to the learner in case application, however, is much less than in firsthand experience. The time period required using the case method to acquire the same amount of knowledge is also normally shorter than it is for firsthand experience.

Solving Marketing Case Problems

The rest of this chapter is devoted to (1) an overview of the most widely accepted, utilized, and recommended problem-solving technique — the scientific method, (2) an illustration case, and (3) an illustrative case analysis.

The Scientific Method

The scientific method is a logical, orderly consideration of the problem situation.[1] In outline form, the sequential steps of the method are:

1. Observation of a situation
2. Statement of the problem or formulation of a hypothesis
3. Discovery and arrangement of facts to allow for prediction
4. Setting up alternatives
5. Selection of an alternative
6. Action or testing of the hypothesis

While there may be some differences in the steps of the scientific method as described by different sources, the method is applicable to most case analysis.

Scientific Method — Application to Marketing
Even though marketing is a social science rather than a "hard" science, the method is applicable, with care, in marketing situations. Hard sciences, such as chemistry and physics, are areas of study where input variables can be identified, measured, and controlled. Moreover, the subjects of study are normally inanimate. In marketing — a social science — the conditions are slightly dif-

---

1. Russell L. Ackoff, Shiv Gupta, and J. Sayer Minas, *Scientific Method* (John Wiley & Sons, Inc., 1962), p. 3.

ferent. Marketing situations usually involve human beings, all the input variables are seldom known, and few accurate measuring devices exist. The degree of control possible with human variables is limited, but some conditions of control can be obtained through research design. For example, the before/ after design, where human subjects are tested before an event and after it to determine their change, allows a limited degree of control. Still, human behavior is not only difficult to predict but also difficult to measure. In addition, measurement may actually *cause* change in human behavior.

Still, the scientific method has advantages which promote its use over other possible methods. For instance, its use tends to minimize uncertainty from lack of information. It also encourages consideration of pertinent facts to the problem. Judgments, too, are more likely to be based on fact than on unfounded assumptions. Accuracy in measurement is a by-product as well.

Alternatives to the Scientific Method

Intuition is an important technique in problem solving. Next to the scientific method, it is probably the most widely used technique. Intuition, as a technique, involves the use of experience with past problem situations to solve present problems. Intuition is quick and overcomes the problems and cost of obtaining data, since the amount of new data used is small. A past situation from which experience was gained may, however, be entirely different from the present situation. Intuition decisions are also frequently hard to justify or test formally before the action is taken.

Other alternatives to the scientific method are the more specialized approaches to problem solving such as linear programming, statistical decision theory and Bayesian analysis. The specialized methods are in fact the result of adaptation of the scientific method to specific situations or the greater emphasis on and sophistication in a particular phase of the scientific method—discovery and arrangement of fact, for instance.

The moral of this discussion is use the scientific method until sufficient experience and sophistication is developed. It gives excellent results.

Illustration Case

The following sample case presents a market selection problem at Douning Sporting Goods Company. It is a good example because there is not a clear-cut decision and it is informationally incomplete. Most problem situations are like this one — informationally incomplete with some information completely irrelevant to the problem. Nevertheless, this case should not be thought of as typical, only as illustrative. That is, there are no typical cases, just as there are no simple formulas for case analysis. Each situation is different; thus, each case analysis must be different. Examination of the Douning Company situation over a period of several years will show that solutions are generated in a dynamic situation. What was successful last year is not necessarily good for this year.

It should be pointed out, however, that a general procedure can be developed for similar types of cases. This is true even though no two cases are the same and case analysis is dynamic. For instance, in the Douning Case, a specific location is not named. It is the specific information, like location or financial ability, which makes each case unique.

It would be beneficial to have all of the specific information to arrive at a solution. But much of an analyst's work is development of a general procedure. This work can be done without the detail. The general procedure identifies important variables and their relationships. Usually, the analyst will also incorporate decision criteria into the general procedure. Thus, even before the specific detail becomes available, the analyst knows both how it will be treated and how it will affect the solution. In the Douning Company Case, the general procedure could be a market selection procedure. One decision criterion might be that a market is not sufficient if its revenue-generating ability is less than $100,000 in a year.

DOUNING SPORTING GOODS COMPANY
Using Marketing Research Results to Market a New Product

In December of 1976, Jim O'Neal, product manager for the Douning Sporting Goods Company of Billings, Montana, was in the process of introducing a new product line into the market. One year prior, in an effort to become more diversified, Jim, along with the company executives, determined that the production and selling of golf equipment could prove profitable to Douning.

Company History

Douning Sporting Goods Company has been in existence eight years. When it was founded, Douning manufactured only one type of snow skis. Since then, Douning has branched out to include a full line of quality ski, bowling, tennis, and camping equipment. In these eight years, the name of Douning has become a leader in quality sporting goods.

During the past five years, Douning has enjoyed a stable profit margin which has remained somewhat higher than the industry norm. Douning feels that this is due not only to the high quality which their products offer, but also to the continuing increase of products in their existing lines and the addition of new products. Douning distributes throughout the United States to major sporting goods chains. Seven warehouses are located across the country which carry ample stock to serve regular needs of the chain stores. The company does not own exclusively any warehouses or retail stores at the present time. In the past year, Douning has set

Submitted by Frank Sabo, Assistant Publications Editor, West Michigan Tourist Association, Grand Rapids.

up manufacturing and testing facilities for their new golf equipment line. Although this new division will eventually supply a full line of golf clubs, golf balls, and golf bags, only the Douning "sweet-swing" golf ball is now ready to market. A tentative advertising campaign has been set up to include advertisements to be run in three magazines—*Golf Magazine*, *Golf Digest*, and *Sports Illustrated*—and also point of purchase displays. Douning is now considering how they will distribute their "sweet-swing" golf balls in an effort to gain a substantial portion of the particular segment of the market they are attempting to reach.

Golf Ball Market

A recent study on consumer criterion for purchasing golf balls was performed for Douning by the Westra Research Company, Minneapolis, Minnesota. This study produced results which Douning believed could be a very useful tool in their decision making.

The study results (shown in Exhibit 1) were tabulated and groupings were made to set up valid correlations. First, the surveys were divided into two groups. Group I consisted of purchasers with a higher golf handicap (nine and above) while Group II were those whose handicaps were zero to eight. The data showed that high quality in a golf ball was an overwhelming factor (92 percent) in the purchase made by lower handicap golfers, while this factor was a minimal influence (21 percent) on higher handicap golfers' purchases. Next, four additional criteria for the purchase of golf balls were measured in both Groups I and II. These criteria were: (1) price, (2) brand loyalty, (3) choice of compressions offered, and (4) the cut-proof feature.

Exhibit 1   *Summary of Data from Golf Ball Survey*

GROUP I *(approx. golf handicap 9 or above)* *In choosing what golf ball to buy —*	*Very important*	*Not very important*
1. How important to you is high quality?	21%	79%
2. How important to you is the price?	84%	16%
3. How important to you is the brand name? (brand loyalty)	28%	72%
4. How important to you is having a choice of compression?	14%	86%
5. How important to you is a cut-proof feature?	83%	17%

In what type of store do you usually purchase golf balls?

Pro shop	*Discount and dept. stores*	*Sporting goods store*
7%	76%	17%

GROUP II (approx. golf handicap 0–8) In choosing what golf ball to buy —	Very important	Not very important
1. How important to you is high quality?	92%	8%
2. How important to you is the price?	72%	28%
3. How important to you is the brand name? (brand loyalty)	76%	24%
4. How important to you is having a choice of compression?	81%	19%
5. How important to you is a cut-proof feature?	10%	90%

In what type of store do you usually purchase golf balls?

Pro shop	Discount and dept. stores	Sporting goods store
78%	12%	10%

Overall, price did prove to be an important factor in both groups (Group I—84 percent, Group II—72 percent), but more emphasis on this was found in Group I. Brand loyalty, on the other hand, was found much more prevalent in Group II (76 percent versus 28 percent in Group I). Further correlations showed that those who chose both price and quality as important factors recorded the highest rate of brand loyalty. In evaluating the effect of different choices of compression, again the data from Group II (81 percent) showed that this was important to them, while to Group I (14 percent) it was unimportant. Conversely, Group I (83 percent) indicated the cut-proof feature of a golf ball to be a prime factor in their choice, while Group II (10 percent) considered this feature unimportant.

The study also gathered data concerning the type of store in which the group studied usually purchased golf balls. Data showed an overwhelming difference between Group I and Group II. Group I purchased the majority of its golf balls (76 percent) in discount and department stores, while only 7 percent were purchased in pro shops. Conversely, in Group II only 12 percent were purchased in discount and department stores, while 78 percent were purchased in pro shops. In sporting goods stores, Group I purchased 17 percent and Group II purchased 10 percent of their totals.

Douning "Sweet-Swing" Golf Balls

The Douning "Sweet-Swing" golf ball is of the highest quality. The "Sweet-Swing" contains a solid India rubber core, which is wound with strips of the purest rubber at high tension. The core and rubber strips are encased in a tough, durable synthetic cover that is painted with a long-lasting white paint. The paint and cover have been tested under extreme conditions and have matched or exceeded the durability of any of the five major competing balls. The

Douning "Sweet-Swing" has been manufactured to comply fully with the standards set up by the U.S.G.A. (United States Golf Association). These standards are that: (1) A ball may not weigh more than 1.62 ounces, (2) a ball must not measure less than 1.68 inches in diameter, and (3) a ball must not have a velocity greater than 250 feet per second, under specified conditions, as measured on the Association's machine. The Douning "Sweet-Swing" is manufactured in three different compression choices: eighty, ninety, and one hundred compressions. The price of the Douning "Sweet-Swing" is $1.20 per ball when purchased in packs of three balls sold for $3.60 per package. All tests of the quality of the Douning "Sweet-Swing" have proven conclusively that it can be a formidable competitor in its particular segment of the golf ball market.

Competition in the Golf Ball Market

There are some forty-two ball manufacturers in the United States. Because the quality of the Douning "Sweet-Swing" golf ball is very high, only a portion of these manufacturers can be considered major competitors. Douning's chief competitors (in order with respect to total dollar sales volume per year) are Titleist Acushnet, Dunlop Maxfli, Spalding Dot, McGregor Tourney, and Wilson Staff. These five companies now represent 58 percent of the total dollar sales of all golf balls in the United States. The quality of the balls which these companies manufacture is very similar, directly comparable to the Douning "Sweet-Swing." These five lines of golf balls are all priced at $1.30 per ball and are packaged in packs of three balls which retail for $3.90 per pack. Additional similarities are that all five lines of balls are manufactured in three different compressions, all five companies manufacture additional golf accessory lines (golf clubs and golf bags), all five companies sell their golf products exclusively through pro shops (golf course or independent), and all five companies advertise their golf products through both golf and sports periodicals. Also, none of the five golf companies is offering the cut-proof feature in the high-quality golf ball line at the present time.

These overwhelming similarities among brands point to the need for a strong quality brand name which will ensure brand preference (loyalty) in the high-quality golf ball market.

Illustrative Case Analysis Comments

In the analysis that follows, note the use of the scientific method. Keep in mind that this is one case, one analysis. As an analysis, it has some particularly good aspects, but also some weaknesses. If the analyst seemingly missed an issue or dealt with one differently than you expected, ask yourself why. Likewise, if an issue was raised which you overlooked in reading the case, ask yourself why.

Student Analysis*

Problems and Observations

The Douning Sporting Goods Company's main problem is deciding which segment of the market it will attempt to capture in order to gain a substantial portion of the market. Once this decision is made, there are other questions that are raised, such as how, when, and where to market the "Sweet-Swing" golf balls. Thorough testing of its own product has established its performance capabilities in relation to the top five competing products, but the survey conducted by the Westra Research Company has discovered that there are two distinct consumer groups with totally different purchasing habits. The methods to be employed in marketing the product will depend greatly on Douning's choice of consumer groups.

According to the survey, Group II is made up of the avid players with lower handicaps. It could be assumed that these golfers come from a higher income bracket than the other groups. They are less concerned with price than with quality. They shop primarily in pro shops which are located only in country clubs and on golf courses.

Group I could be classified as the once-a-week golfers. They do not have very much leisure time for practicing golf, hence their handicaps are higher. They would probably be from a middle-income bracket. They are concerned with price and usually buy at discount and department stores.

Evaluating the Alternatives

There are three possible target markets that the Douning "Sweet-Swing" golf ball can appeal to: Group I, Group II, or a combination of both groups.

1. The Mass Market: There are some risks involved in trying to appeal to both groups. It will probably end up that one group will buy more than the other. If the difference in sales is large, the money spent on trying to reach the group that bought the least would have been wasted. There would have been a great deal of useless advertising, unnecessary production, and inefficient development of market channels. But in appealing to

---

*Mary Jane Fitzgerald and Howard Moerdyk, Principles of Marketing students at Western Michigan University, Kalamazoo.

both markets instead of one, the new product's exposure to the golfing public is greater. The product does have features appealing to both types of golfers.

2. The Avid Golfer Market: The company may choose to appeal just to Group II. This strategy also has a great deal of risk involved with it. The "Sweet-Swing" golf ball has not yet established itself in the good-quality market, thus Group II will be hesitant to try this ball. The strong brand loyalty in this group may prove to be an asset, once Douning is the recognized quality leader. If a golfer is also active in other sports for which Douning manufactures equipment and is satisfied with these products, he/she may chance trying the ball. However, an avid golfer may seldom spend time on any other sport. The "Sweet-Swing" golf ball has a new cut-proof feature that helps save balls, but this feature does not concern Group II. They have lower handicaps, consequently their swings are better, more consistent, and less likely to cut the ball. The price, however, may appeal to this group. The "Sweet-Swing" is $.10 per ball and $.30 per package cheaper than competing balls. The last feature mentioned in the survey, compression, should not make a difference in sales, since the leading brands are all comparable.

3. The Duffer Market: Group I is the last target market analyzed because it appears to be the most profitable choice of the three. Group I is not concerned with quality, brand name, or compression. The biggest risk that Douning has in introducing the golf ball to this market is failure because, being a new product in a developing line, it has not established itself. Another possible reason for failure is Douning's past distribution policy. Douning has been distributing its products through major sporting goods chains while golfers in Group I probably buy most frequently at discount outlets. Moreover, Douning has not proven its good quality, although it does have a successful brand name.

   These drawbacks to potential sales in the Group I market may not be as influential as other aspects, however. The two aspects in the survey that concern this group are those of price and the cut-proof feature. These golfers are primarily of the middle-income bracket. Having a higher handicap, they probably use and/or lose more balls, thus having to buy more. It can be assumed, then, that they look for lower-priced balls and are not concerned with quality. The new cut-proof feature is an important advantage from this group's perspective, since the ball will last longer and, ultimately, cost less.

Selecting an Alternative
Of the above three alternative marketing choices, number three— the higher handicapped golfers—seems best for Douning's marketing effort, primarily because a golfer in this market is concerned about the cut-proof feature and the price and is not particularly resistant as a result of brand-name loyalty. This group is also most likely to be the largest at the present time due to a general increase in leisure time, the recent popularity of golfing, and the current stress on exercise and physical fitness. This group also has the greatest potential for improving its golfing handicap and thereby becoming more concerned with other features such as quality and choice of compressions. This growing product appreciation would also tend to create a potential market for the other golf equipment to be introduced by Douning at a later date.

Implementing the Alternatives
The next concern is strategies for reaching this market. Golfing is a seasonal, warm weather sport. The advertising and sales campaigns should begin in March, rather than January, when the golfing season is about to begin nationally and when the impact would be closest to the actual initial purchase time. Another possibility would be to have the campaign concentrated in states where the climate is warm all year. The campaign might be started in the fall months in warmer climates and, if the product does well there, advertising could be introduced during the spring months in those states that have snowy, cold winters. This approach would cut down on overall cost and serve as a broad test market.

Because the survey shows that Group I buys primarily at discount and department stores, Douning should concentrate the distribution of the "Sweet-Swing" to these places of business. Great emphasis should be placed on point-of-purchase displays, for eye appeal can be a big factor, even in selling an item such as golf balls. It would be advantageous to have introductory display stands in public golf-course pro shops. Golfers of both groups go into these shops, whether to buy or to browse. A display or poster with a list of where the ball is available would expose it to public golfers of both survey groups.

From the survey taken, it is hard to determine whether a magazine advertising campaign would be effective or not. The survey should have included a question concerning sports publications read. These magazines usually include tips on "how to improve your game" and information on professional players and tournaments. Very avid golfers would probably be the ones to subscribe to this type of publication, probably members of Group II. They would also have the money to spend on these magazines. If Douning wished to advertise in magazines, this new product might be introduced in advertisements for sporting goods sold in other magazines that concern themselves with sports in general, the assumption being that middle-income people would be more likely to subscribe to one of these magazines instead of specialized ones, feeling they would be getting more diversified information for the money. Attempts should be made to convince one of the magazines to do an article on the new cut-proof feature offered by Douning on the "Sweet-Swing." This would be a nonadvocate source of advertising which people would be more likely to take seriously as news than as advertising.

Another possible approach is television advertising. Spot announcements during televised sporting events—such as tennis, golf, and bowling—would be especially good. Such advertising is expensive, however. Because of this cost, television advertising should probably be used only during the introduction phase.

The product's high quality and other features should encourage repeat purchases once it has been tried by the golfer. Because of the product's potential to generate repeat purchases, introductory pricing should be used. As an introductory offer, four balls for the price of three could be the offer. Sampling should also be considered as a technique for getting the product into consumers' hands.

Finally, an effort should be made to obtain pro golfer endorsements—preferably endorsements from golfers who, despite their smaller stature, are known for their long ball. It is a commonly held belief that the distance a golf ball is driven is a function of the size of the golfer; so, by using golfers of smaller stature, more attention would be focused on the importance of the ball in the drive. Endorsements from both men and women should be used. The emphasis of the endorsement would be on both their long drives and on their lack of concern about cutting the ball in the occasional edge hits they make in hitting the long ball.

It is very important that all advertising be coordinated, each type reinforcing the other and presenting the same image of the product. Certainly, the distribution system should be sure to have the product available for purchase once demand is stimulated. Distribution must also be coordinated with advertising.

Through all these channels it should be possible to reach Group I. Emphasis should be put on the ball's low price and on the new cut-proof feature that will also save money.

REFERENCES

Books and Articles

Bolt, Gordon, "Seven Marketing Lives of your Product," *Marketing Times* 21, no. 4 (October, 1974), pp. 8–10.

The Conference Board, Inc. *A Guide to Consumer Markets* (New York: The Conference Board, Inc., 1974/75).

"How Acushnet Plays to Win at Golf," *Business Week,* February 17, 1973, pp. 90–91.

Mandell, Maurice I., *Advertising,* Englewood Cliffs, New Jersey: Prentice-Hall, Inc., 1974.

"New Products: Building a Winning Momentum," *Sales Management,* October 1, 1969, p. 52.

"New Products: The Push is on Marketing," *Business Week,* March 4, 1972, pp. 72–77.

U. S. Bureau of the Census, *County Business Patterns,* 1965.

Personal Interviews

March 7	Interviewed the "Pro" at Elk's Club
March 8	Interviewed the Sporting Goods Department Manager at Meijer's, a discount chain
March 14	Interviewed Mr. Lee of Lee's Sporting Goods Store

Preparation for Good Case Analysis

A good solution or good analysis does not just happen; a solution must be nurtured in a favorable atmosphere. Descartes' advice on problem solving back in the seventeenth century suggests that part of the favorable atmosphere is mental. His four principles of problem solving were:[2]

1. Put all preconceptions out of mind. According to the analysts in the illustrative analysis, they initially set aside a three-hour

---

2. Rene Descartes, *Discourse on Method* (Chicago: Henry Regnery for the Great Books Foundation, 1949).

block of time in which the case analysis was their only concern. At the beginning of this period, they carefully read the case trying not to form any judgments, only familiarizing themselves with the information in the case.

2. Break the problem into its parts. This can be seen in the Douning case as a series of questions: What market, media, and distribution?

3. Solve the easy parts first. Ease of solution is sometimes determined by order or sequence, as in the Douning analysis. The market, distribution, and then media problems were solved in order.

4. Make sure everything has been included. The analysts of the Douning case indicate that they wrote their analysis, put it aside, came back to it two days later and checked it for completeness.

Frank Alexander Armstrong also recognizes the mental aspect of a favorable atmosphere. This top marketing executive's description is very clear and helpful.[3] In brief, he says that mentally the best problem solving takes place when the mind is free of other thoughts, inquisitive, and able to work without outside interruption for an extended period of time.

Pitfalls in
Problem Analysis

Certainly there are a number of valid reasons for having difficulty in solving marketing problems. But a valid reason in one situation may only be an excuse in another situation. The best strategy is to know what these reasons are and to make sure that they are reasons instead of excuses.

The excuse heard round the world is that there is not enough information. Decisions very often are made without 100 percent of the information desired. The amount of information *required* is a function of the amount of risk one willingly accepts. The more information available, the less risk there should be. Risk is a part of marketing/management. Nevertheless, if more information is needed, specify that information precisely and keep in mind that acquiring information and analyzing it requires expenditure of resources. For instance, in the Douning illustration, it was noted that the survey by Westra Research had not included needed questions on sports magazine readership. This being noted, the

---

3. Frank Alexander Armstrong, *Idea-Tracking* (New York: Criterion Books, Inc., 1960), pp. 139–44.

analyst made assumptions which allowed suggestion of a solution in the area of media selection.

Another occasional pitfall is the desire to eliminate making assumptions. Assumptions are necessary; but they should be well-justified assumptions, rooted in fact. Such assumptions are most likely to be valid. If several assumptions seem equally justifiable, determine their effect on the outcome by trying them one at a time. Play the "what if" game by asking: What if this was not an assumption, but a certainty? How would the analysis and conclusion change? In the selection of the duffer market segment in the Douning analysis, the analysts used both fact and assumptions in their interpretation of the facts. One such assumption was that the duffer loses more golf balls and thus would buy more "Sweet-Swing" balls.

Another pitfall is hedging or refusing to make a decision on what the solution should be. The ultimate objective in marketing case analysis is to arrive at a solution. Unless a decision is made on what the solution should be, the analyst has fallen short.

The last pitfall to be discussed here is failure to justify. The analyst searches for *the* perfect answer. Few marketing problems, however, have only one correct answer. More than one answer can be correct if they are justifiable. A justification includes the logic, facts, and expert opinions behind the decision, assumption, or solution. Well-justified and substantiated solutions are more likely to result in equally acceptable outcomes than are unjustified decisions. Seek out experts, test the logic and facts used by exposure to other analysts, and substantiate by referring to experts. The references at the end of the Douning analysis indicate effort to justify, substantiate, and test the logic and facts used.

CONCLUSION

The case and analysis presented in this chapter are illustrative rather than typical. You perhaps can see where you would have done things differently, which is as it should be. All the case situations you encounter in the coming chapters have possible solutions. You will find the process of problem solving—of looking for answers to a problem—has some universal elements which should carry over from one setting to another, and you should become a better problem solver with each problem you solve.

chapter

2

Marketing Management and Decision Making

SNO-GO TRAILS
A Recreation-Related Franchise

Early in October, Rico O'Connell purchased a snowmobile for his personal use. It was only after much deliberation that he had decided on making the investment (slightly over $1,200), given the newness of the sport; yet, from his personal observation, snowmobiling seemed to be a rapidly growing pastime. Rico was a resident of Watertown, New York, a small town located in a year-round recreational area in northern New York. Snow depth suitable for snowmobile operation was not common until late in December. However, Rico was able to obtain a 10 percent discount for buying the snowmobile prior to the start of the season.

Shortly after purchasing his snowmobile, Rico read an advertisement in a magazine offering franchise opportunities for snowmobile rental businesses. Although more curious than interested, Rico sent to the address listed in the article for more information. What he received was a brochure explaining the status of Sno-Go Trails of America, Incorporated, and several attractive features of a Sno-Go Trails Franchise.

Statement of Status

Sno-Go Trails of America, Incorporated, is engaged in meeting the increasing demand of the American public for recreational outlets, more particularly in the winter sport of snowmobile outings. The recreation business is on the threshold of unprecedented growth. Sno-Go Trails is in the operation of snowmobile rental.

Submitted by Kiven Graves

Franchisees of the company specialize in providing a pleasant outlet for this recreational market, advertising themselves as Sno-Go Trails. Much goodwill for the business and public acceptance is being generated in the operation.

In return for the franchise fee of $7,500, Sno-Go Trails of America, Incorporated, agrees to qualify and train the franchise owner, approve a location, and acquire operating equipment (five new SL 338 Yamaha snowmobiles). In addition, the franchise owner is required to pay the company 8 percent of gross sales from the rental of snowmobiles, the minimum sum based on gross revenues of $600.00 per week. This royalty amount of 8 percent of gross sales was allocated as 7 percent general royalty and 1 percent as a fund for national advertising. Further, a guarantee was placed on the 1 percent of gross sales assessment for national advertising which stated that the 1 percent would not be increased, and that if the franchiser's advertising expenditures did not equal the amount collected, a prorated return would be effected.

Information Rico Acquired

Although Rico was unfamiliar with the operation of snowmobiles, he felt that this would not necessarily be a hindrance to entering the business, since the sport of snowmobiling was rather new. He had also noticed a heavy influx of tourists bringing snowmobiles with them on their trips north during the last winter sport season. Many of the trailers carrying the snowmobiles had identifying numerals on them typical of those found on rental equipment.

During the prior season, three franchises had been in operation. The locations were Green Bay, Wisconsin, Racine, Wisconsin, and Allendale, Michigan. Since Allendale had the weather conditions most similar to Watertown and was within a reasonable distance, Rico decided to talk to the owner of that particular franchise. He was able to determine that the franchise had experienced a rather limited success. The owner had collected gross receipts of slightly over $11,800 during his first season of operation (three months), thus paying back the original investment of $7,500, plus other expenses, and showing a profit of $1,625.

Rico felt that since Watertown generally ran a longer winter recreation season and offered far greater resort facilities, he would be able to exceed the volume of business of the Allendale franchise.

Prices for snowmobile rentals were set by the franchiser at $8.00 per hour or $5.00 per half hour per snowmobile. The trend,

Exhibit 1   *Profit statement — Allendale, Michigan Franchise*

Expenses

Franchise cost	$ 7,500
Local advertising	400
Land rental	800
Gas and oil	250
Maintenance and repair	125
Liability insurance	300
Payroll	700
Miscellaneous	100
Total	$10,175

$11,800	Cash receipts
10,175	Expenses
$ 1,625	Profit

however, was toward the hour rental with over 90 percent of all riders spending $8.00. There was no extra charge for two people riding on one snowmobile. In addition, the dealer had purchased a snowmobile sled to accommodate young children which was also available at no extra cost.

Rico was able to find some old national figures on the number of snowmobiles. In the 1962–63 winter season, 10,000 units were in operation. By 1968, yearly sales had risen to 200,000 units, a 200 percent increase over a five-year period. Sales projections in this source indicated 300,000 units to be sold in 1969, with the figure rising to well in excess of 500,000 units in 1970 (no later figures were available).

Renting a machine provides a desirable alternative to purchasing a machine, because the cost of a snowmobile (ranging from $600 to $1,400 for popular models) excludes a vast potential segment of the market which would participate in weekend outings but find the initial cost prohibitive.

The rented land could also be used to provide trails for those who already own a snowmobile but do not feel quite adventurous enough to risk a breakdown on the typical isolated trails available to the public. Since snowmobilers generally travel in a group, those who own snowmobiles could pay a nominal fee ($1.50 per hour) to use the trails while their friends would be able to rent a snowmobile at the same location without the necessity of expensive weekend rentals or transportation costs.

Since the concept of renting snowmobiles is obviously a service which cannot be patented, a franchise is not required to enter the business. The advantages of purchasing a franchise instead of entering the business as a sole proprietor include:

1. Entering the business under the relatively new, yet established name of Sno-Go Trails.
2. Furnished advertising mats.
3. Assistance in location selection.
4. Furnished signs and banners.
5. Business set up and made operable by the franchiser.

Disadvantages of entering a franchise agreement as opposed to entering the business as a sole proprietor include:

1. Large initial cash outlay.
2. Commitment of 7 percent pure royalty (excluding 1 percent for national advertising).
3. Contract necessitates operation seven days per week and establishes sales quota ($600 per week).

Liability considerations play little part in the decision-making process, for the contract contains a hold-harmless clause to negate any liability on the part of the franchiser. Although the legality of hold-harmless clauses is currently under question, the franchisee is established as an independent contractor, a fact which further removes the franchiser from any judgments resulting from accidents (in excess of liability insurance in the amount of $300,000).

Machinery breakdowns are of extreme importance in the rental business, since the loss of one machine for one day could very easily effect a $100 loss. The main source of breakdowns of snowmobiles in the Allendale franchise was drive belts burning out. To alleviate this problem, it is possible to eliminate the extra strain put on the belts by eliminating the use of the tow sled. The sled is not featured in the advertising, nor is there an additional charge for it. Therefore, eliminating a tow sled should not affect the number of customers or revenues.

Machines have a useful life expectancy of 1,000 hours of operation. To relate this to expected usage, each machine would be in operation approximately 300 hours per season, and should last for three seasons before replacement is necessary.

Fixed costs total $8600 for the first year of operation. During the second season, fixed costs will drop to only $1100, since the franchise cost is not amortized.

The franchiser, in addition to setting up the business and approving a location, reserves the right to inspect the records kept by the franchisee and to inspect the premises and equipment at any time. In addition, sale of the franchise is subject to approval by the franchiser.

The franchiser, according to the terms of the contract, offers a protected area with a radius of three miles from the franchisee's location. Although three miles seems small, it could indeed prove valuable in densely populated tourist areas.

Although a rudimentary knowledge of common mechanical difficulties and safety factors is desirable, no special training would be required.

The franchiser is a subsidiary of Recreation Resources of America, Incorporated, an Iowa corporation with assets in excess of two million dollars.

For the first season of operation, approximately $10,000 would have to be realized either through invested capital or through sales generated from the initial cash outlay.

Although the Allendale franchise experienced only a $1,625 profit, this would increase greatly were the franchisee to liquify the assets. The snowmobiles are the property of the franchisee and after one year of depreciation still retain a value of $500 to $600 each. Thus, an additional profit of $2,500 to $3,000 could be realized if the franchisee did not wish to resume operation. However, if he does desire to remain in business, the following year his fixed costs will drop $7,500 with a resulting soar in income, even on the assumption that sales did not increase as expected. Although a rise in maintenance costs may be expected, expensive repairs are unlikely since the major components of the snowmobile carry a twenty-four month warranty. Also, preventive maintenance can be initiated during the off-season to minimize the possibility of loss of revenue due to mechanical breakdown.

The prospective franchisee should not wait to see more long-range results, for the critical period of operation is the first season. Therefore, little could be gained by observing second- and third-year operations. In addition, with such an enormous rate of growth of the overall snowmobile industry, competition is undoubtedly not far behind. It sounds pretty good, but Rico has not yet made a decision.

Questions

Should Rico invest in a Sno-Go franchise?

What marketing factors should he consider? How does each influence the desirability of the franchise?

Construct a pro forma profit statement for the first year's operation of Rico's franchise.

CAR-PED COMPANY
Making the Most of an Opportunity

Car-Ped Company recently acquired an exclusive right in its industry to use the style and names of various models of cars produced by General Motors, Chevrolet Division. Car-Ped is the first firm in its industry ever to be granted such a right by General Motors. Management must decide on how to capitalize on this agreement.

Car-Ped Company is a manufacturer of children's pedal cars. The manufacturing headquarters is Tot, Illinois. The company manufactures items in the product categories shown in Exhibit 3.

Exhibit 3   *Product categories and price comparison*

	Car-Ped price	Competitor's price — Kid's Kars		
		California	New Jersey	New York City
Pedal autos	$24.00	$22.50	$24.00	$24.00
Pedal tractors	19.00	19.00	17.00	17.00
4-wheeled wagons	9.00	8.50	9.00	8.00
Push scooters	7.00	7.00	6.00	7.00

*Prices do not include shipping $1/1,000 miles.

The previous year Car-Ped was the leading manufacturer of wagons, second in pedal tractors, ninth in push scooters, and twelfth in pedal autos. The pedal auto has the fastest turnover and

---

Submitted by Robert D. Rose, Jr., Sales Representative

highest profit. Sales were made on a nationwide basis, but there were many highly populated areas with no Car-Ped outlets. The uneven sales can be seen easily in Exhibit 4.

Exhibit 4   *Car-Ped's market share*

	Car-Ped share	Total kiddie riding products
California	$ 69,000.00	$2,000,000.00
Illinois	394,050.00	1,500,000.00
Indiana	185,000.00	1,000,000.00
Iowa	24,000.00	700,000.00
Michigan	800,000.00	1,600,000.00
New York	86,500.00	2,000,000.00
Ohio	132,000.00	800,000.00
Texas	28,000.00	750,000.00

Car-Ped's products are of good quality. Their overall pricing structure is comparable to most other firms with the exception of Kid's Kars, which prices its pedal autos slightly below Car-Ped's. However, Car-Ped is at a disadvantage in markets such as California because of transportation costs. Toy retailers in the distant states find it more profitable to deal with manufacturers in that area. A car shipped to California, for example, will have a $3 transportation cost included in its cost to the retailer.

Distribution is handled by the major types of retail outlets shown in the accompanying table.

Retail outlet	Percent of dollar volume
1. Department stores	35%
2. Bicycle shops	30%
3. Toy stores	20%
4. Mail-order houses	15%
5. Discount houses	0% *

*In consideration

Department stores are the first-choice outlets largely due to prestige, large sales volume, and willingness to carry Car-Ped's full line. Discount houses are becoming quite popular, but it is Car-Ped's policy not to sell to them because of their direct competition with the department stores.

Sales territories are divided by state boundaries with one salesperson per state, in most cases, except California which has two salespeople.

The advertising budget for the previous year was about 3 percent of gross sales. A total of $128,000 has been budgeted for this year, appropriated as shown in the accompanying table.

Advertising Budget

Direct mail to retailers	$12,000.00
Newspapers	17,000.00
Cooperative dealer ads	9,000.00
Consumer media (mostly magazines)	61,000.00
Art and copy	15,000.00
Displays	14,000.00

The arrangement with General Motors included a $7,000.00 down payment and a 4 percent royalty on all sales using General Motors styles or names. General Motors also has the right to approve such products and advertisements used and made in connection with their name.

Car-Ped realizes the possible benefits of using the General Motors name. Car-Ped also sees the need for further promotion and consumer awareness in California. However, promotional funds are extremely limited. On the other hand, there seems to be an excellent opportunity to influence customers favorably with advertising (particularly those in California).

Questions

How should Car-Ped promote its products?

What channel(s) of distribution should it use?

How can it best take advantage of its exclusive rights to styles and models of Chevrolet?

GOOD TIMES PARTY STORE
Developing Strategy in Pricing

In 1962, a party store, Good Times, was opened by Stacy Kreber, a very competent owner and manager. The store was located in an excellent location with easy access and a large demand for this type of store. The party store was located on a heavily traveled main artery of Concord, New York; thus much of the business was derived from the location alone. As time progressed, the party store became known as the most complete party shop in town. It sold all party needs, including beer, wine, groceries, snacks, ice, frozen foods, produce, sundries, and — most important — liquor. By 1967, the store was the number one wine shop in town, and second in liquor sales. Every wine imaginable was available, as well as any liquor the customer might want. A number of people also patronized this store because its beer selection was complete: imported beer, all local premium and regular brands, and keg beer. Taking all into consideration, the store was number one in all respects.

At the time Good Times was showing its largest sales and return on investment, a nearby neighborhood party store, Quick Trip, was slowly diminishing in popularity and sales. Whether the lack of sales was due to poor management, some other internal problem, or competition, was not known. At any rate, Quick Trip was slowly going downhill, and carried less and less of what the customers wanted.

Submitted by Richard Rossol

The owner of Good Times was an adventurous person and wished to sell out at quite a profit. With this in mind, a well-organized projection of the profitability of the store was taken by a supermarket chain, which then purchased Good Times. The store then became one of a chain of convenience stores. Soon, all convenience grocery items were added to the fine selection of wines and spirits. Impulse-shopping items were displayed and an excellent job of merchandising was done. The operating hours were lengthened for shoppers' convenience—7 AM to 11 PM every day, including all holidays except Christmas.

The first year's profit projection was not only met, but exceeded by a substantial amount. Quick Trip had, in the meantime, closed its doors and was for sale. The supermarket management contemplated buying the neighborhood store, but chose not to make an investment so close to one of its member stores. Months later, Quick Trip was opened under new ownership and management by Kreber, the previous owner of Good Times. A complete physical face-lifting was done, and a very new modern interior was completed. Now being modern, completely remodeled and very efficient, Quick Trip posed a threat to Good Times. Its owner and backer had intentionally aimed to cut into Good Times' business. The newly remodeled Quick Trip was just as complete as Good Times in every way. Its hours of operation were the same and neighborhood patronage was very heavy.

Two more liquor-selling party stores also had recently opened in the neighborhood. Needless to say, the competition was becoming very intense. Quick Trip and Good Times were very similar now in all ways except two. First, Good Times was owned by a chain operation, theoretically giving it more power and a financial advantage; and, secondly (surprisingly), Quick Trip was exceedingly low in retail prices. They were so low that they were in direct competition with a discount supermarket chain. The beer and wine prices were, on the average, $.30 per six pack of beer lower than those at Good Times. Grocery items were also priced much below competitor's items of the same type.

The profit margin or mark-up picture in convenience stores is generally quite standard. A minimum of 16 percent mark-up on beer and wine must be made to pay operating expenses and manpower. No return on investment will be realized at this percent. The mark-up (on retail) of 33⅓ percent is a normal profit for convenience stores of this nature. All wine is 33½ percent, imported wines 40 percent, beer 25 percent, and all groceries approximately 33⅓ percent. The new Quick Trip, however, was selling beer and wine at a 9 percent to 10 percent mark-up and groceries at 15 percent. Their prices were definitely beating the competitors', but theoretically they could not survive in business. After six months, Good Times realized that Good Times' business had dropped from $15,000 sales weekly to $13,000 weekly. In some instances, on holidays and special occasions, an even greater decrease was noted. The manager of Good Times kept track of the number of cases of liquor delivered to Good Times and those delivered to Quick Trip. He noticed an increase at Quick Trip and a little decrease at Good Times. He concluded that Quick Trip was not making the profit margin of Good Times, but it was doing an equal volume in sales. He also noticed that many of the new customers gained when Quick Trip was originally closed were no longer trading with Good Times.

Trying to overcome this decrease in sales volume and profit, Good Times management tried reducing the price of its best-selling wine to match Quick Trip's price. After a month's observation of sales, no sufficient increase in volume was noticed, so the price was accordingly readjusted. Since this time, management has not tried anything further to correct or slow down the rate of sales decline. They have resigned themselves to the fact that Quick Trip is definitely hurting their business, but have also resigned themselves to the fact that they can not obtain all the retail party store business. Moreover, management for Good Times is also convinced that the return on investment is less than normal at Quick Trip and eventually Quick Trip's management will revise prices upward.

Question

> *Establish marketing objectives, strategy plans, and control procedures for Good Times.*

FRANK SUD FURNITURE
Changing a Distribution System

Frank Sud Furniture is one of the many small companies that abound in the furniture industry. The plant's value is approximately $15 million, and it employs 186 people in management and production.

Established in 1893, by Frank Sud I, the company has always dealt in high-priced, custom-made furniture. The ·market is relatively small, but profitability is high, especially since most furniture companies have now gone to mass-production techniques and products. Only a handful of the custom manufacturers now exist.

Remaining in Portland, Oregon, Frank Sud Furniture has expanded three times since its inception. In 1923, under Frank Sud II, the capacity was doubled in response to the "roaring twenties" spending. In 1943, after the death of Frank Sud II, Frank Sud III foresaw the postwar "boom" in the furniture industry and expanded once again. Also under his direction, Tower Furniture, an across-the-street neighbor, was purchased in 1949 to almost double once again the productive capacity of Frank Sud Furniture.

Sales have traditionally been carried on by a very limited number of "high-class" furniture outlets and company salespeople-decorators. This allows Frank Sud Furniture almost complete control over both the marketing and production processes. The stores work through a very small inventory, supplemented by company catalogs. The company sales force works mainly through

Submitted by William VanManen, President, Mikioi Metalcraft, Honolulu these same catalogs, with the stores and with individual interior deccrators. The company supplements these efforts with a large showroom in Seattle, Washington, and by participating in various expositions across the country throughout the year. This type of sales structure is considered to be the most expensive by most furniture manufacturers. The forty national salespeople average $32,000 per year and the eight expositions cost $12,000 per show. This is equal to approximately 9 percent of net sales. The extremely high selling expense is justified by Mr. Sud as necessary to maintain the image of the company's fine line of furniture.

Recently, however, Mr. Sud has been entertaining the possibility of changing his marketing structure. Offers from fine furniture stores and showrooms have been forthcoming regularly for years but have usually been rejected on the grounds that Mr. Sud himself would lose control. However, two large, established showrooms recently contacted him in reference to handling his product.

One, Sud Showrooms (no relation) of New York, with five showrooms on the east coast, has been increasingly persistent. With approximately thirty excellent decorators per showroom, it is one of the highest calibre showrooms (and competitors) in the east.

The second one, Knife and Tubes, has showrooms in Chicago, Dallas, Los Angeles, and Denver. With approximately twenty-five decorators per showroom, this would give Frank Sud Furniture more coverage in large cities "west of the Mississippi."

Both companies have offered to assimilate the present company sales personnel in their respective areas, and both have agreed to show substantial amounts of Frank Sud Furniture in all of the furniture expositions each attends.

Mr. Sud has spoken with Kristen Ludlow, marketing manager, and John VandonBrank, production manager, and has asked them to come to his office to discuss all possibilities.

Questions

What channel(s) of distribution should Frank Sud use? Why?

THE SEVEN BROTHERS CORPORATION (A)
Application of Decision Tools—Product

Incorporated in the state of California in the year 1962, The Seven Brothers Corporation, with its head office in Los Angeles, was one of the medium-sized manufacturers of sailboats in the United States. For many years the company sales increased steadily. The boat the company produced was sold under the brand name of LUCKY. The company relied primarily on independent dealers for retail sales. Most of these dealers were located in the resort areas on lakes and beaches. The sales records of the company showed a seasonal pattern which was translated by the company researchers into a seasonal index, as shown in Exhibit 5.

Exhibit 5   *Seasonal sales index*

Northern United States		Southern United States	
Spring	1.20	Spring	1.15
Summer	2.25	Summer	1.50
Fall	.50	Fall	.80
Winter	.05	Winter	.55

The sales for 1968 were forecasted as $1,600,000 for northern United States and $4,800,000 for southern United States. Due to keen competition in the industry, the company decided to set up dealers' contests in both the northern region and the southern region. The budget for such a contest was 1 percent of the fore-

Submitted by Kung-Mo Kuo, Ph. D., Assistant Professor of Business Organization and Management, The University of Wisconsin—Platteville

casted sales for each season in each region. Since this was the company's first trial, it was decided that continued use of contests was to hinge on the success of the initial contest. "Success" means an increase in sales — specifically, 10 percent increase over what was projected for each region and each season; for an increase in sales of over 6 percent would result in an increase in net profit that would more than offset the contest expenses. The actual sales for 1968 are shown in Exhibit 6.

Exhibit 6   Sales for 1968

Northern United States		Southern United States	
Spring	$472,000	Spring	$1,250,000
Summer	910,000	Summer	1,990,000
Fall	190,000	Fall	940,000
Winter	12,000	Winter	600,000

As a result of the analysis made on the dealer's contest, such a contest was continued only during the summer season for southern regions for the year 1969.

In 1969, the marketing manager, John Grimm, retired and the new marketing manager, Kate Anderson, took over. Since Anderson took over, company sales have declined slightly and profits have remained at the 1968 level, $650,000. The company is considering replacing Anderson, who has become uncooperative and occasionally belligerent. Management sees three possible options:

1. Get a personnel search firm to locate a replacement.
2. Hire a replacement by use of classified ads in the national paper.
3. Retain the present Marketing Manager, Kate Anderson, for a little while.

The personnel search firm indicated a 50/50 chance that they could find a top-notch replacement with the requirements set by the company. The cost of the recruiting methods, the probability of the replacement's success by each method, and the resultant effects on profits before taxes are shown in Exhibit 7.

Had the personnel search firm not been able to find a replacement, the firm would either hire through classified advertisement or retain the incumbent manager.

In 1970, the company was lucky enough to hire Jack Robinson, a college graduate with five years of experience in the sporting goods manufacturing business and the outboard motor business. Under the new leadership, company sales started to pick up again.

Exhibit 7   *Recruitment method information*

Recruitment method	Cost	Probability of replacement's success	Effect on profit*	
Personnel search firm	2,000	0.9	If successful	+40,000
			If not	− 5,000
Classified ads	500	0.6	If successful	+10,000
			If not	−10,000
Retain	0	—		0

*Recruiting costs not included

Unfortunately, in the latter part of 1973, the sales of the company dropped sharply (25 percent), due to the energy shortage. With his background in the sporting goods business, Mr. Robinson was contemplating a proposition to alleviate the company situation as it was at that time. The idea was to diversify company business into "pinpool" tables which can be used for both ping pong and pool, using convertible edges and reattachable hard carpet with movable patches that cover the holes. The following new equipment is needed to diversify in this direction:

500 small special electric hand tools	$100,000
50 special designer's cutting machines	$150,000

The estimated depreciation for the new tools and other costs are:

Depreciation for new tools	$ 20,000
Depreciation for building	$250,000
Administrative salaries, sales expenses—direct* and other overhead costs	$147,000
Variable expenses (labor cost, material cost, etc.)	$ 50 per pinpool table

*All salespeople are on straight salary

The maximum production capacity is about 20,000 pinpool tables per year. It was estimated that the pinpool table can be sold at the wholesale price of $80 to retailers. The market for pinpool was estimated as way over 20,000 pinpools for the state of California alone.

Mr. Robinson's idea was accepted by the president of the company, Mr. Jim Morgan, and soon the "pinpool" will be scheduled for further planning. Knowing that promotion for the new product is the key to success, Mr. Morgan advised his marketing researchers to study this matter. As the result of the study of a sales history of a medium-sized sporting goods firm that sells both ping pong tables and pool tables, it was found that the following relationships exist:

$$P = \$100S + \$80A$$

where: S = Sales presentation
               A = Ad insertion in *Sports Illustrated*
               P = Profit before taxes
with a correlation coefficient of 0.955

It was also estimated that for each sales presentation, twenty hours is needed, and for each ad insertion in *Sports Illustrated*, twenty-five hours work is involved. Each sales presentation will cost $100 and each trade paper insertion will cost approximately $50.

With the total company hours for sales personnel limited to 5,000 hours and budget limited to $20,000, Mr. Robinson, the marketing manager, had determined the optimal promotional efforts — namely optimal sales presentation and ad insertion for the pin-pool. Of course, the optimal promotional program has to be geared to the intended market which Mr. Robinson also has already mapped out.

If you were the executive officer of the Seven Brothers Corporation, you would have made the following decisions:

1. Decision on the continuation or discontinuation of sailboat dealer's contest in each region and each season for 1969.
2. Decision on the replacement of the "disenchanted" marketing manager.
3. Decision on pinpool business proposition — the "go" decision.
4. Decision on the optimal promotion program of the firm regarding the pinpool operation.

Questions

How did you make these decisions? Suggested approaches to the solutions of the decision problems:
For decision problem 1: seasonal index analysis
For decision problem 2: Bayesian or decision tree method
For decision problem 3: break-even approach
For decision problem 4: linear programming

chapter

3

Marketing Information-
Research Cases

HEMLOCK HILLS
How Much, What and How: Marketing Research

Hemlock Hills is a ski area located near Plainwell, a small city in Michigan. It is twenty miles northeast of Kalamazoo, a larger city of approximately 80,000 population, from which it draws most of its clientele. It has been in operation for ten years, and has grown substantially from its state on opening day in December, 1961. This is the first year, however, that the owners have actually made money from it: prior to this year, all profits have been reinvested in the operation for development and expansion.

Hemlock Hills was started with total capital of $10,000 — $1,000 of which was put up by the two owners, Bob and Tom Jones, and the remainder of which was financed through bank loans. There has not been any outside investment in the business. When it was opened, it consisted of two natural hills of intermediate caliber, one rope tow, and a small lodge (600 square feet). The hills required little work except tree removal. Two tickets could be purchased for $3.00 on weekdays and $4.00 on weekends, and equipment rental — skis, boots, poles, and breakage insurance — was $4.00. The owners, who are brothers, did all the building, maintenance, and development of the hills and facilities themselves, and have continued to do so.

Starting and developing a ski area is a very risky and difficult venture. It often takes several years to get the business going successfully. So, despite a first-year net loss of $2,850, the Jones' brothers continued work on the improvement of the hills and facilities and advertised it more extensively prior to the opening of the 1962–63 season. This second year proved to be more success-

Submitted by Stephanie Richards

ful, due to good snow conditions throughout most of the winter and increased patronage, and a net profit of $3,675 was realized (after payment of the owners' salaries).

Over the next eight years, work on the area was continued. During this period, a total net profit of $26,400 was realized, all of which was reinvested. The quality of the skiing offered improved substantially with the addition of eight hills, eight rope tows, and one Pomalift. The new hills include one fairly long intermediate slope (700 feet), which is the only hill accessible through use of the Pomalift; three steep, advanced hills, with elevation of over 1,200 feet, and the bottom portions of which are also used as intermediate hills; two beginning-intermediate slopes, one long beginning hill (800 feet), and one trail through the woods. The caliber of skiing offered by Hemlock Hills is now very good in relation to the terrain (quite flat) and is becoming increasingly competitive with the other ski areas within a fifty-mile radius.

The lodge facilities have also been expanded. The lodge, which is situated at the bottom of Oak Run, the advanced hill, now occupies 2,000 square feet on three levels. The main floor contains the equipment rental room (400 sets of rentals), the ticket office, the offices of the manager and ski school director, an instructors' meeting room, a cafeteria and eating area, and a lounge with a fireplace. The ground floor contains a basket rental and a room for putting on ski boots, and so on. The upper floor contains a bar which faces the hills, and a large ballroom and bar, used for dances on Friday and Saturday nights. The management has succeeded in attracting some non-skiers to these social activities, and would like to increase this clientele.

At present, Hemlock Hills employs one Ski School Director, one full-time instructor, and nine part-time instructors. In the past three years, enrollment in Ski School classes has increased rapidly. A special four-week ski school, sponsored by the local newspaper, has had a very good turnout, with enrollment of over 2,500 people in the past two seasons. This has led to a substantial increase in the number of skiers in the area, and in the number of people who patronize Hemlock Hills. Also, in the past two seasons, the area has entered into agreements with a university and a college for the use of the area for physical education classes, available to students at special rates. This has proved very profitable and has led to increased use of the area by students.

Another activity which has been sponsored by Hemlock Hills and has been successful are snowmobile races on Wednesday nights and on special weekends. There are a large number of snowmobilers in the area, and further development of this activity could bring additional revenue.

By next year, the owners plan the addition of two more hills and a chair lift. One of the present steep hills is going to be lengthened to about 1,700 feet, which will be a great improvement. Also under consideration at present are the development of a golf course for use in the summer and the building of overnight lodging for out-of-town patrons.

The firm is interested in the cost of marketing research to find out whether their present or potential market would warrant additional development of the hills and the other recreational projects possible. For instance, if they built overnight lodging facilities, would they have enough out-of-town skiers using them to make it profitable? They would like to know if it is feasible to develop the ski area into a resort. This is a very difficult question to answer, and one which would require analysis of the present market segment that Hemlock Hills holds and of the potential market they could gain. The owners would have to be assured of patronage from the surrounding states of Illinois, Indiana, and even further south, where skiing is impossible. Although Michigan skiers usually go to northern Michigan for ski weekends, those less-advanced skiers from the more southern states where skiing is rare may well be attracted to Hemlock Hills, because it is much closer than the bigger and better resorts of northern Michigan. It must also be taken into consideration that the snow conditions in Michigan are not the best; a good base may often be ruined by a January thaw — right in the middle of the season! Also, the season here is much shorter around Hemlock Hills than it is further north; February rains are usually the end of the skiing, and it is impossible to count on much spring skiing in such an unpredictable climate. Whether or not other recreational facilities could be developed is a question that would also require research into the potential market.

Another question about which the owners are concerned is advertising. They have previously used very little advertising and have relied primarily on word-of-mouth advertising within the area. However, if Hemlock Hills were to expand to resort dimensions, they would probably have to undertake extensive advertising. Again, the question of where and how much to advertise would require some study.

To answer these questions Hemlock Hills' management is willing to spend between $2,000 to $3,000 over a four-month period. The study should at least give them an idea of the feasibility of further expansion and development of the area. It would be helpful for them to know their maximum potential market and to what degree they could expand with some assurance of support.

Another question which could be answered by research is that of the most profitable pricing schedule. At present, the cost of tow tickets is high for the quality of the skiing offered by the area. For example, it is possible to ski Boyne Mountain in Michigan, which has much better hills, for the same price. However, smaller ski areas like Hemlock Hills usually have to charge higher prices to compensate for the smaller crowds that patronize the area. In

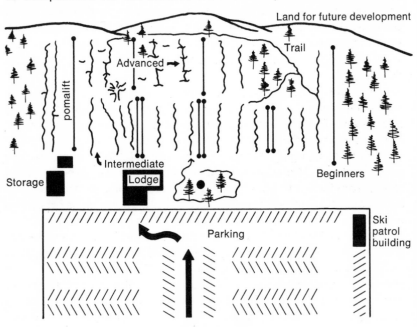

Present hours	
Monday through Friday	1:00 to 9:30
Saturday and Sunday	10:00 to 5:30

Planned hours for 1976–77 season	
Monday through Sunday	10:00 to 10:30

Tow fees	
Weekdays	$ 3.75
Weekends and holidays	$ 5.00
Season pass	$90.00

Rentals	
Skis	$2.00
Boots	$2.00
Poles	$1.00
Package (including insurance)	$4.00

other words, Boyne is able to charge the same price for much better skiing because they have such large drawing power among skiers.

One final question which could be answered through research is that of hours. There must be enough people buying tow tickets to pay for the overhead involved in running the tows, lights, opening the lodge, and so on. It is impossible that they could offer special rates during slack hours to attract more people. For example, Ladies' Day on Wednesday has been very successful. Tow tickets, rentals, and instruction are all half-price, and many women with free time during the day have been prompted to take up skiing because of this offer. Similar offers might encourage patronage by other groups — children, students, etc.

Question

> Write a research proposal for Hemlock Hills management which will answer their most important marketing questions. Include cost figures, a questionnaire (if used), etc.

NICKLES DEPARTMENT STORES

There has been a strong feeling among some retailers, particularly the mass merchandisers, that the stores must be open when customers want to shop, not when the store's management or personnel want to be open. Some mass merchandisers have extended normal daily shopping hours to include late hours every night of the week and Sundays.

Changing buying habits have encouraged retailers to push for Sunday openings. Some states, however, do not permit opening on Sundays. Other states have relaxed local laws. Some department stores have begun to follow the discounters' lead and have remained open for business on Sundays.

In one recent year there was more temptation than ever to open on particular Sundays. Christmas just happened to fall on Monday. Traditionally, the shopping day before Christmas has produced huge volume for most stores. Nickles Department Stores, a retail chain in the South, faced a problem of whether this particular Sunday before Christmas their stores should remain open. Up until this year they had rejected the "open Sunday" proposals.

It has been said that department stores may soon be forced to open on Sunday in order to suit customer convenience. The greatest argument against Sunday openings for Nickles' is that even under six-day schedules, there is a problem finding enough personnel. The caliber of sales personnel is low enough without stretching the supply still further.

Submitted by Gilbert R. Boersma

Typical of Nickles' managers was the reaction of Terry Lasich, the Atlanta store manager: "I would try my very best never to have to work on Sundays, even if I could take off any other day of the week. If we stayed open, the additional hours would be too costly, and it would not be fair to my staff to work so many hours. I would not hire additional salespeople for an extra day."

It was the general opinion of the board of directors for Nickles Department Stores that, if they were to consider opening stores on Sunday, it would be done with reluctance by certain area stores. They doubted that a situation which would force Nickles to open on Sundays would develop.

Several states, like Massachusetts and Pennsylvania, have "blue laws" that would prohibit Sunday openings. However, these laws are generally regarded as out-of-date and on the way out; in Georgia, a court recently struck down state blue laws.

On the other hand, there have been definite signs of a movement to cut back retail hours in the face of what has been the opposite trend. Some store managers say they would rather give good service for five days than operate six days with staggered personnel. Some ask, "How can we attract top personnel when retailing has the bad image of long hours and low pay?"

The management of Nickles Department Stores has noted that store employees could be given two-day weekends by staggering schedules. Nevertheless, customers ask for specific salespeople, people they know, and of course, the training of part-time help is not easy.

An Interview

In an interview, the President of Nickles Department Stores answered the following questions:

1. Why would Sunday be an excellent shopping day for customers and retailers? Sunday would be an excellent shopping day for customers because it is not a working day and they would have time to buy the things that they have been meaning to. It would also be convenient, if the day before Christmas should be a Sunday. The retailers would benefit from the probable increase in volume due to the lengthening of shopping days. But one must realize that when Christmas lands on Monday, Saturday is considered the last shopping day. Giving the customers the opportunity to shop Sunday may not lengthen the shopping period, but instead allow the shopper to put off last-minute buying one more day.

2. How does the retailer overcome the argument that "the additional hours would be very costly in terms of overtime to sales personnel who are overworked already"? The retailer can overcome this argument by simply giving employees two-day weekends on staggered schedules. Several problems may develop from the use of this method, however: customers may not get desired service, more part-time help may be needed, full-time help may be unwilling to work weekends, and proper sales coverage may be impossible due to a less dependable sales force.

3. Should state legislation permit those retailers who want to remain open on Sundays to do so — in other words, permit freedom of choice? I feel that state legislation should permit retailers to have freedom of choice on whether to stay open on Sunday or not. Each retailer must be responsible to the needs and wants of customers and be able to respond to them. Legislation against opening on Sundays would merely be oppressive.

4. Would downtown stores benefit from Sunday openings as much as suburban stores? The answer to question 4 may be found if a survey is taken to answer question 1. Within the survey, one would more than likely be able to pick out two subsamples: (a) shoppers of the suburban stores and (b) shoppers of downtown stores. I believe it would be found that they would benefit equally, although there may be some disapproval from the downtown area because of church activities. Let it be noted that the answer to both questions 1 and 4 may be found in secondary data, which would eliminate the need for a survey.

5. Could retailers best serve the shopping needs of their customers by staying closed on a weekday and staying open on Sundays? To close on a weekday and open on Sunday would best serve the shopping needs of the customers only if it was found that a particular day during the week was costing the store too much to remain open and that the customers desired to shop on Sunday. Each store within the chain would have to determine their own particular situation, in order to make the best decision on this matter.

6. Would stores increase their sales if they remained open Sundays or would they merely sell the same amount of merchandise, but stretch the sales out over a longer selling period? This sixth question is particularly difficult to answer, even with the use of research. During an increased shopping season, such as Christmas, it is probable that sales volume would have a chance to increase. It is possible during a normal week of sales

that volume would increase also, since a certain segment of the market would have more time to shop. But the lengthened buying period may only give the customer better selection of shopping time, with no increase in the total spending for the period.

7. Since Sunday is the day before Christmas this year, does this justify opening the store? A survey of customer opinion may answer this question. As previously stated, though, the opening of the store on Sunday before Christmas may not lengthen the buying period, but make Sunday the day for last-minute shopping instead of Saturday. The Sunday before Christmas has traditionally been filled with church functions celebrating this special religious holiday. Most churchgoers would have no time or desire to shop on a day that brings out the true meaning of Christmas.

8. What influence does religion have on the final decision of some stores? I would think, as indicated in the last answer, that religion would have a great influence on the decision to open stores on Sunday before Christmas. With the exception of those religions which do not call Sunday a special day of worship, religion may still influence the final decision of whether to open on Sunday throughout the year. If there is no objection on the part of the customers to a particular store, or the store employees for that matter, and there is a desire or need to be open on Sundays, that store may then decide to open. Even in this case there would still be religious influence on the hours a store would be open on Sunday. Generally, stores open on Sunday will be open only for the afternoon hours because of the morning and evening worship services that many churches hold.

Research

The managers had recently come across a study on Sunday shopping. The research was conducted in a nearby town of approximately the same size. Four hundred patrons of enclosed malls were interviewed. These interviews were conducted on two consecutive Sundays in each mall during normal business hours, 1:00–5:00 PM. Interviewers were assigned a specific, but different location in each mall during the interviewing period. They were instructed to interview the first person walking past their position at ten-minute intervals. In the city where this research took place, Sunday openings have been allowed for a number of years. But, except for a few discounters, retailers were generally closed on Sundays. When the enclosed malls were built they started from the beginning with Sunday openings.

The data from the research report are shown in Exhibits 1 through 7.

Question

> What conclusions could managers draw from the research and apply to the Atlanta store?

Exhibit 1   *Selected characteristics of 400 Sunday shoppers*

Sex	Percentage	Shopping group	Percentage
Male	37.7	Alone (single)	11.0
Female	54.1	With friend	33.4
Unclassified[1]	8.2	With family	53.4
		Unclassified	2.2

Family income	Percentage	Age of household head	Percentage
Under $8,000	21.2	Under 25	21.0
$8,000–$12,500	31.7	25–34	22.2
Over $12,500	24.9	35–49	27.2
Other[2]	22.2	50–64	19.2
		65 and over	7.7
		No answer	2.7

Community size reared in	Percentage
Under 5,000	20.2
5,000–50,000	21.5
50,001–100,000	19.7
Over 100,000	21.5
Other[3]	17.2

1. One interviewer inadvertently did not classify the respondents by sex. However, other cross-classification by sex did not indicate that the "unclassified" category would substantially alter this relative percentage of females and males in the sampled population.
2. "Other" in the table includes the respondents who did not know family income and interviewees who refused to answer.
3. "Other" in the above table refers to interviewees who were reared in several communities of various sizes and interviewees who refused to answer.

Exhibit 2   *Main reason for shopping today*

Reason	Percentage*
To look around	44.7
To make a purchase	36.9
To see a special promotion	7.3
To dine out	7.0
To visit a particular store	4.2

*$N = 385$. Fifteen respondents were unable to answer this question or refused to answer it.

Exhibit 3   Amount spent on Sunday shopping trip
              by shopping group

Amount spent	Responses
Under $5.00	104
$5.00–$9.99	52
$10.00–$24.99	67
$25.00–$49.99	25
$50.00–$99.99	10
$100.00–$499.99	4
$500 or more	1
Don't know[1]	19
No purchase[2]	118
TOTAL	400

1. 19 respondents were unable to estimate amount spent by their shopping group as the group had scattered.
2. 118 respondents had made no purchase at the time of interview. A purchase might have taken place after the interview.

Exhibit 4   Shopping plans and purchases

	Purchase planned product		
Product category	Did	Did not[2]	Total[1]
Clothing	76	104	180
Notions	32	33	65
Food/groceries	19	28	45
Home improvements	5	15	20
Appliances	3	3	6
Furniture	2	4	6
TOTAL	137	187	324

1. Indicated plans to shop in this category. Of the 76 respondents who did not plan to shop for any particular product, 10 respondents did purchase at least one item.
2. This should be interpreted to mean the planned product had not been purchased prior to the interview. It does not mean that the shopping group has not purchased "unplanned" products.

Exhibit 5   Day of week usually shopped by
              frequency of Sunday shopping

	Day usually shop		
How often shop Sunday	Monday–Saturday	Sunday	Total
Less than once a month	50	7	57
Once a month	128	35	163
Twice a month	51	37	88
More than twice a month	57	64	121
TOTAL[1]	286	143	429

1. Some respondents selected more than one day.
2. $X^2 = 46.56$; df = 4; $p < 0.001$

Exhibit 6   *Frequency of shopping by information source*

	Information Source			
	Advertising	*Driving*		
How often shop Sunday	*media*	*past*	*None*	*Total*
Less than once a month	20	5	32	57
Once a month[1]	59	26	52	137
Twice a month	51	12	31	94
Three times per month	8	8	8	24
Every Sunday	45	10	27	82
TOTAL	183	61	150	394

1. Six respondents who shopped once a month refused to reply. $X^2 = 20.24$; df = 8; $p < .01$

Exhibit 7   *Frequency of Sunday shopping related to response on pleasantness of Sunday shopping*

	Sunday shopping pleasant change from weekday shopping			
			Doesn't	
How often shop Sunday	*Agree*	*Disagree*	*matter*	*Total*
Less than once a month	16	10	31	57
Once a month	75	14	54	143
Twice a month	67	9	18	94
More than twice a month	75	6	25	106
TOTAL	233	39	128	400

$X^2 = 37.33$; df = 6; $p < .001$

SEATONE DEALERS
Price Cutting

The Seatone gasoline dealers in Gotham City are having a problem with competitive gas pricing with the other dealers. Until this year, there had been little price cutting in this city. With the advent of many new independent dealers, price wars have been on the increase. From September 1 until November 1 alone, there have been three wars.

The greater Gotham City area has a population of about 100,000, served by 232 dealers of both major and independent brands. Seatone has the largest share of the gas market, with twenty-one stations in this area. This amounts to 9 percent of the total dealers, with approximately 15 percent of the total gasoline sales. All of the Seatone dealers offer regular car maintenance service and also sell a complete line of automobile accessories.

Seatone Oil Company, the local Seatone distributor, and the local dealers are seeking the most profitable alternative in dealing with price cutting by the other dealers. The present policy agreed upon by all three levels is that for every $.01 the price is dropped, Seatone Oil Company absorbs $.004 loss, the distributor $.003 and the dealer $.003. The Seatone dealers, in a stable market, sell their regular grade at $.769 per gallon. After deductions have been made for dealer cost and federal and state taxes, the dealer is left with a $.05 per gallon margin, with which all overhead must be covered and a reasonable profit allowed for.

Normally, the independents sell at a price $.01 to $.02 lower than the major brands, which price the latter tolerate. It is when jobbers, buying overproduction at distressed prices, resell to independents on a narrow margin, that the independents sell at a lower price to increase their volume. This is when the gas war begins.

Of course, the Seatone dealers do not rely totally on gas sales for their revenue. Approximately 30 percent of their volume comes from TBA (tires, batteries, and accessories) and 20 percent from maintenance and minor repairs. The remaining 50 percent is derived from the sale of gasoline. However, 62 percent of the profit is derived from the 30 percent volume from TBA and 20 percent maintenance and repair revenues. The independents, on the other hand, rely almost totally on their gasoline sales for their revenue.

During past price wars, Seatone's prices have, on occasion, dropped to $.689, with the independents at $.669 to $.679. At a $.689 price, the Seatone dealers have only $.026 margin. Since their break-even point is estimated to be at a $.035 margin, they are incurring a loss on each gallon sold.

The first question which has been raised is what will happen if the Seatone dealers maintain their normal price, regardless of what others do. From past experience, and available reliable data, it has been shown that, when the independents drop their price to $.03 or more below Seatone's, price consciousness supersedes brand preference and Seatone's gas sales suffer.

The effective use of trading stamps has also been discussed as an alternative by the dealers. About 9 percent of the major and independent dealers in this area presently offer stamps with gas purchases. However, none of these offer multiple stamps on a day-to-day basis. Therefore, the Seatone dealers have considered using a multiple-stamp offer as an alternative to price cutting. Seatone Oil Company's policy is to subsidize 50 percent of all multiple-stamp costs. Since this is, in effect, a price cut, and since the oil company is absorbing 50 percent of the cost, it appears to be a feasible and less expensive alternative to a price cut. Another advantage of this plan is that the independents often do not respond with lower prices to these multiple-stamp offers. However, its effectiveness is limited to about a $.03 price drop by the independents.

Since the Seatone dealers offer TBA, maintenance, and repair service, they may be able to use this as an effective tool in drawing in more business to cover their losses in gas sales during a price cut by the independents. This would require covering the market with sufficient advertising both through local newspapers and radio. The expense of the advertising, through agreement, will be allocated as follows: Seatone Oil Company — 25 percent, local distributor — 25 percent, dealers — 50 percent. For an effective campaign, it has been decided that a quarter-page advertisement in the local newspaper should be run in the Sunday edition, at a total cost of $225. A series of 10-, 20-, and 30-second spot commercials on radio, run during the week of the sale, will cost $300. With the 62 percent profit margin derived from this area, the Seatone dealers should have a definite advantage over the independents, who do not offer these lines.

Give-away promotions and self-liquidating items, such as nylons and soft-drink six packs sold at a less than retail price, have been used with varying degrees of success by other dealers. Since the self-liquidating items seem to be valued more by the public, and since they even provide a small profit, they seem to be the better of the two choices. Since the latter can be handled at no cost, it can be used even in place of the stamps. These are effective, as are the stamps, only to a certain margin in prices.

The installation of car washes at the stations, with reduced rates to large-gallonage buyers, may also be used to draw business back from the independents. However, besides the large initial installation fee, a problem encountered is which stations will get the car washes. If all twenty-one dealers got them, there would probably be an excess of car washes in Gotham City. The Seatone organization is wondering if a non-price-conscious market exists. In order to find out, they have decided to do a survey of the market.

Question

Prepare the questionnaire for this survey.

chapter 4

Market Identification and Measurement Cases

MID AMERICA PAPER COMPANY
Product Mix and Forecasting

The Mid America Paper Company has operated in a small town between Detroit and Chicago since 1909. In its sixty-seven years of existence, Mid America Paper Company has moved up from a one-machine mill to a complete paper-making and finishing operation. The mill now contains two high-speed paper machines that have the capability of producing 150 tons per day per machine. The mill does complete roll finishing and has a new, completely automated sheet-finishing operation.

In its sixty-seven years of operation, Mid America Paper has grown with the United States paper industry. It manufacturers fine printing papers for books, advertisements, and converting. Production of paper has increased over the past twenty years on an average of 4.2 percent, which is just under the industry average of 4.8 percent[1].

Since 1969, Mid America Paper's profit margin has been declining rapidly. The financial statement for the second quarter of 1971 reported the first loss in the company's history. Since the start of the decline in 1969, Mid America has been tightening up on all facets of its operations, but the paper industry has been suffering from increased costs and low prices. The recession has hurt the industry, especially the small paper mills like Mid America.

Management's View of Mid America Paper

Management feels that the company is doing everything possible in the mill to increase production and lower costs. All sorts of

---

Submitted by William Roschek, Sales Representative, Georgia Pacific, Kalamazoo
1. "Beset by Overcapacity, Paper Firms to Limit Near-Term Additions," *Wall Street Journal,* November 11, 1971.

controls have been incorporated at Mid America. The company has increased production from 125 tons per day per machine to 150 tons per day per machine. This increase in production was necessary to offset the rise in material and labor costs, because the marketplace would not accept higher prices.

The plant runs seven days a week because the loss of production will drastically hurt the profit picture. The increased production, however, is not moving out of the mill fast enough. Inventories have built up from the standard 4,900 tons to 6,500 tons. The stocking program has become too cumbersome, because the company has not been able to sell the paper. Management feels it is necesary to get the paper sold soon and not carry more than 4,900 tons; overstocks are too much of a burden to the company.

Management is seeking a different strategy in the marketplace to increase the sales volume and increase the prices. The increase in sales volume would keep the machines running seven days a week and reduce the inventory. It is anticipated that a price increase of $10 per ton will maintain profit at the mill. Unfortunately, low demand in the market precludes such an increase.

The Product

Mid America Paper supplies a large variety of paper for offset and letterpress printing. Exhibit 1 is a list of standard grades and current prices from Mid America Paper.

To keep both paper machines running seven days a week for 339 days,[2] at least 103,700 tons of paper must be sold. Of this, 11,000 tons will have to be sheeted to keep the finishing room running. The prices are in line with the industry, and the market has enough potential for the 103,700 tons.

The Market

The market consists of paper merchants (wholesalers). Mid America sells directly to these merchants who, in turn, sell the paper at a 2 percent markup to the printers. The paper sold to merchants is usually shipped directly to the printer's warehouse.

Because of its location, Mid America's sales force of five salespeople and a manager concentrate on the Detroit and Chicago markets and the encompassing area fifty miles around each city.

---

2. Downtime includes six holidays and twenty maintenance days.

Exhibit 1   *Paper offerings and price*

Grade	Basis weight[a]		Price/ton[c]
Computer Bond Wh.	30½	#	$250.00
	34	#	250.00
	38	#	225.00
	46	#	220.00
	51	#	218.00
Form Bond Wh.	30½	#	255.00
	38	#	250.00
	45	#	248.00
	51	#	246.00
	61	#	248.00
	71	#	248.00
Form Bond Colors[b]	25½	#	308.00
	30½	#	304.00
	34	#	302.00
	38	#	298.00
	45	#	294.00
	51	#	288.00
	61	#	290.00
	71	#	290.00

a. Basis Wt. equals the weight of a ream of paper (500 sheets) in the size of 25″ × 38″.
b. Colors include pink, blue, yellow, and green in all shades.
c. These prices are for roll items only. For sheets, $15.00/ton is added.

The sales manager believes that the New York marketplace holds much potential for Mid America and would like to make a deeper penetration into this market.

The sales forecast for the upcoming year is shown in Exhibit 2 by grade of paper and tons. This forecast was done by executive opinion.

The sales territories are covered by two salespeople in Chicago and two in Detroit. The other sales personnel and the sales manager service other markets in the midwest and the New York area. Selling expense is 15 percent of sales. The sales manager believes that the two biggest job facing the sales force are selling the right grades of paper effectively and lowering the selling costs. The manager also believes that the sales department can easily attain the required sales; but, before developing sales quotas and expense budgets, more should be known about the New York market. There is not complete agreement with the sales manager's assessment of the situation. The confusion which does exists is demonstrated by fragments of conversation from the latest executive committee meeting.

Exhibit 2   *Sales forecast*

Grade	Basis wt. (in lbs.)	Tons
Computer Bond Wh.	31½	6,900
	34	6,900
	38	7,200
	46	6,900
	51	6,900
Form Bond Wh.	30½	6,900
	38	6,900
	45	6,900
	51	6,900
	61	6,900
	71	6,900
Form Bond Color	25½	2,500
	30½	3,400
	34	3,400
	38	4,900
	45	3,400
	51	3,400
	61	3,400
	71	3,400
TOTAL		104,000

Eavesdropping on an Executive Committee Meeting

"The problem facing us is to determine the right product mix to attain the maximum dollar sales volume while satisfying customer demand and keeping the paper machines running."

"The target market is all paper merchants in the Detroit, Chicago, and New York paper markets."

"The best approach to solving the problem is to look at the marketplace and see what products are in the greatest demand; then concentrate on selling these products."

"A detailed evaluation of every account should be made. If this is not available, we should look at trends in the industry as far as what type of paper is most in demand by printers."

"Market indexes will give us an idea of how the industry is doing and if there is enough potential."

"The demand for our products is a percentage of the total printing paper demand. Any printer that needs this type of paper will be our potential customer."

"A test market is needed to determine if we can raise the price $10 per ton."

"It is rather doubtful that prices can be increased. The national economy is bad. High inflation and a recession are evident."

"Our competitors are all paper mills that produce fine printing papers for offset and letterpress printing."

"How our competitors are making it I don't know."

"The growing market is mostly in New York. All markets will be growing but not as fast."

"We should try to sell colors and sheeted paper because they have the best selling prices."

"If prices can not be raised we should especially try to sell more colors and sheeted paper."

"Since everything possible has been done in the mills to curb costs and increase efficiency, a bad product mix must be the reason for the loss."

"More colors should be sold and less white paper. The forecast shows more white paper planned to be sold."

"The sales forecast shows a poor product mix."

"Whether we attempt to go into the New York market should depend on the information gathered in research."

"Our sales force may not be able to cover the whole market. If deeper penetration into the New York market is wanted, more salesmen should be employed."

"The printing industry is directly affected by the national economy."

"If they can get the right selling price, an increase in colors and sheeted paper should help us get back into 'black figures.'"

"Executives' opinion is a quick way to forecast sales, but it is more guesswork than scientific evaluation. A better way would be to have each salesperson give a composite picture of his territory. Another available way is projection of trends. Both of these methods are more scientific and may point our deficiencies in our marketing strategy."

Questions

What forecasting technique should Mid America use?

What market segment should be emphasized? Why?

CLAYMORE SPORTING GOODS COMPANY
Establishing the Direction of Future Growth

Mr. John Claymore, Jr., has been president and chief stockholder of the Claymore Sporting Goods Company for the past six months. He moved into this position after his father, John Claymore, Sr., died of a heart attack. Not only did he take over his father's position, but he also inherited his father's stock, which was 53 percent, enough for controlling the company.

Before moving into the job as president, John Jr. served as vice-president and chief advisor to his father for two years. Before that he had received master degrees in both business management and business marketing at a large midwestern university. He graduated with honors from this school, as well as being a super star on both the varsity basketball and football teams. For many years, he has had a keen interest in sports as well as business.

John Jr. got along well with his father and had a lot of respect for him — in both business and in their personal lives. But he often had the feeling that his father was too conservative in trying innovations in the sporting goods business, thus restricting the potential growth of the company. His father seemed to listen intently to his ideas on how the company could grow, but tended to make little use of most of them.

The company had been started in 1945 by John Claymore, Sr., and Carl F. Tremont in Lima, Ohio. The original name was Claymore and Tremont Sporting Goods Company. These two men went into business as equal partners. They both invested $20,000, and set up production in a small wing of an old warehouse in the center of the city. They hired fourteen employees who mainly sewed basketball and baseball uniforms. To a lesser degree, they

Submitted by Mark Hitchcox

also made tennis, track, and gymnastic uniforms. Some of the heavy sewing was done by machine, but the majority of the sewing at the time was done by hand.

In the beginning, Mr. Claymore and Mr. Tremont did most of their own promotional work and made most of the sales. As business grew and their market expanded, a small sales staff was set up, not only to handle sales but also to do the promotional work. More equipment and production employees were also added.

As business continued to grow and sales expanded, the company began to purchase items from other sports equipment manufacturers — such as footwear, basketballs, footballs, baseballs, tennis balls, scorebooks, and many other miscellaneous gear needed in interscholastic sports — to supplement their own line of sporting goods. Generally, these goods were carried as a convenience to the company's retailers, as there was not much profit made from them.

By 1962 the business had grown so much that a new plant was built on the outskirts of the city. The location was ideal for receiving and shipping, being located near the railroad and a new modern highway. The new plant had the potential of tripling the production rate of the old warehouse plant.

Shortly after the new plant was in operation, the company again expanded its personnel. Production employees were increased from forty-one to fifty-eight; field salespeople were increased from eleven to sixteen. Actually six new field salespeople were hired as one of the original eleven moved up to regional sales manager, a position created to supervise the enlarged sales force.

The market had grown from a section of western Ohio to include all of Ohio, Michigan, Indiana, and sections of northern Kentucky, and sections of northern and central Illinois.

In January of 1963, Claymore and Tremont decided to sell stock in the company in order to enlarge it even further. Between them, they retained 53 percent of the stock in order to maintain control. The new stockholders were mainly from the Lima area, and they had their meetings on a quarterly basis. The majority of the money gained from issuing stock was used in payment of some of the large debt owed on the new plant and the purchase of more equipment needed to increase production and replace worn-out equipment.

In November of 1963, Mr. John Claymore, Sr., bought out his old partner, Mr. Tremont, for $125,000. Mr. Tremont had been in ill health for the past couple of years and had decided to retire.

Business for the company grew fairly steady for the next few years as Claymore expanded the market even further into the states already mentioned. By 1971, however, this growth had tapered off and held steady until 1974, when a sharp decrease in sales and profits took place.

John Claymore, Jr., felt this was partly due to his father's conservativeness and inability to change with the times. For instance, John Jr. felt that the style of modern sports uniforms leaned toward the "flashy" type with all kinds of swirls, multicolors, racing stripes, etc. He tried to convince his father before his death that they should produce such uniforms to keep up with their competitors. His father disagreed, and they continued to produce the plain uniforms, similar to the ones produced in 1945.

Another factor that John Jr. thought held back growth was that the business was oriented toward selling to retailers who sold mainly to high schools and, to a smaller degree, to colleges. He felt this had been a good strategy in years past, as Claymore's products were high-quality and the goods bought to supplement their own line were also of high quality, but in today's markets this arrangement made the company inflexible.

The company seemed to be missing out on a lot of business in areas such as little league baseball, small-fry football, as well as adult recreation leagues, where top-quality, expensive equipment was not always feasible. John Jr. believed these kinds of organizations had grown a lot since 1945 and should be part of their marketing program.

Another criticism John Jr. had of the company was that the advertising procedures for the company's products had been too restrictive. For the most part, advertising was done in magazines that were oriented to coaches and athletic directors of interscholastic athletic programs. To a small degree, sports pages of local newspapers were used, but generally this was done on an infrequent basis. He felt the company's products needed more recognition, an increased product identity, and this could be done mainly by increasing the amount of advertising.

Mr. Claymore, Jr., realized that his company is relatively small and there is a limited amount of capital available for the objectives he has in mind. Therefore, it must be decided in which areas they should attempt to implement a plan that will give the best results for their dollar and get sales going again.

To begin the decision-making process, John Claymore, Jr., called a special meeting of his staff to discuss some of the key items. Claymore's present organizational chart is presented in Exhibit 3. The staff meeting was made up of members shown on the organizational chart. Special meetings were hardly ever attended by the stockholders.

Exhibit 3   *Organizational chart*

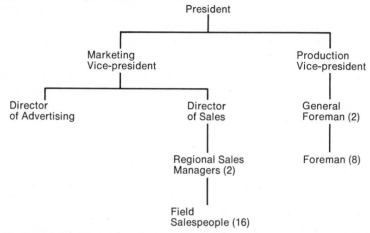

President

Marketing Vice-president

Production Vice-president

Director of Advertising

Director of Sales

General Foreman (2)

Regional Sales Managers (2)

Foreman (8)

Field Salespeople (16)

Some of the key questions raised at the staff meeting follow:

1. Flashy styles of uniforms and their potential
   a. What is the current trend and projected trends of flashy styles of athletic uniforms?
   b. If the trends appear favorable for enlarging our market, how much investment in additional equipment will be needed to produce the uniforms?
   c. Because the Michigan area accounts for a large amount of sales, what effect will the following ruling, passed by the Michigan High School Athletic Association, have: all athletic uniforms must be plain enough to make numbers on the uniforms clearly visible to the game officials. This rule went into effect September, 1973.
   d. What are the possible chances of other states' rules committees adopting rules similar to the one in Michigan?

2. Production of a lower-grade product
   a. What is the potential market available in selling less expensive types of sporting goods oriented toward little leagues, adult recreational leagues, etc.?
   b. To what degree has the competition already saturated this market?
   c. What is the possibility of getting our current retailers to handle a cheaper line of goods?
   d. Will it be necessary to sell supplementary products of lower quality by purchasing them from other producers, in the same manner as quality equipment to supplement our own quality products is purchased at present?

3. Possible change in the advertising program
   a. What changes in advertising are needed to give our products better coverage?
   b. Do the current sales warrant a raise in the advertising budget?
   c. Should advertising be oriented more toward the whole regional market, or toward the local market of the individual retailers?
   d. What other types of advertising media should the company consider?

Mr. Jack Myers, company vice-president and marketing head, organized a small committee consisting of himself, both regional sales managers, and three of the field salespeople to run a thirty-day research project to answer the questions.

An interview was held with Ms. Bailey Phillips, supervisor of the Sporting Goods Department of the L. W. Holzwarth Department Store Annex in Battle Creek, Michigan. Ms. Phillips described how her store handled mainly top-quality goods, serving primarily high school athletes and coaches in the area. Since moving her department to the new annex, other lines of equipment as well as expensive equipment could be sold through the store. Although the department has been in the annex only a short time, she is very pleased how well these new lines have sold.

In another interview, Mr. Tim Gordon of Jack Hopkins Sporting Goods Store, a store dealing with high-quality sporting goods, felt that getting involved with lower-grade products would hurt the reputation of his business. He believes that most of their business comes from repeat customers and on the recommendation of other customers, and that only a high-quality line of products could sustain this reputation.

With regard to the questions, the committee concluded: getting the proper equipment to produce the flashy uniforms would have been reasonably feasible, but the rules committees of other states favor the Michigan ruling, and might be expected to follow such a ruling in doing away with the flashy uniforms because of the confusion of seeing numbers. This ruling appeared to have its influence on many coaches and athletic directors who were interviewed, as many had gone back to the plain uniforms or indicated they intended to do so in their next orders.

It was discovered that the competition in the lower-quality sporting goods market is much greater than in the higher-quality goods market. Nevertheless, many of the company's current retailers showed a great amount of interest in handling a lower-quality type of product as well as the high-quality ones. The sale of the less-expensive lines would not hurt sales of the existing products;

these products are generally purchased by two different types of consumers.

If Claymore goes into the production of the lower-quality goods, a supplementary line of lower-grade products bought from other producers would not be needed, because these products have already saturated the market very heavily and are easily attainable by all retailers.

For the types of products Claymore sells, and for the market it sells to, advertising in magazines oriented toward coaches and athletic directors as is presently the practice is well warranted.

The type of consumer who purchases from Claymore Products already has a knowledge of it from an earlier use or from recommendations from reputable sources. It is believed that more promotional work in the field by the field salesperson is needed more than a change in the current advertising procedures.

It was also discovered by the committee that the Michigan Senate has permitted girls to participate in noncontact sports at the interscholastic level, and has already scheduled a statewide meet for gymnastics. The U.S. Department of Health, Education and Welfare has also recently made rulings regarding the necessity of giving equal opportunity to women in sports activities. In the new developments such as this, it is extremely important for the field salesperson to gain the attention of those involved and responsible for getting equipment for these new programs.

Future plans should be set soon.

Exhibit 4   *Statement of earnings for the year ending December 31, 1975*

	1968	1969	1970	1971	1972	1973	1974	1975
Net sales	$424,358	$489,508	$626,460	$721,887	$873,845	$900,092	$898,000	$710,000
Costs and expenses	367,320	405,177	527,670	608,647	704,274	759,767	758,000	628,000
Depreciation and amortization	9,831	8,071	10,294	11,243	16,936	18,928	19,000	21,000
State and local taxes	4,227	5,224	6,283	7,939	10,425	19,199	16,500	12,500
Income from operations	42,977	71,035	82,213	94,057	97,209	109,478	104,500	48,500
Other income	2,125	2,302	1,855	3,453	3,159	3,159	4,200	4,200
Other expenses	1,235	1,622	1,998	6,934	6,771	6,772	5,120	3,500
Earnings before federal income tax	43,867	71,715	82,071	90,576	93,600	104,403	103,580	49,200
federal income tax	19,200	36,650	42,050	46,600	47,400	58,600	57,500	20,800
Net earnings	24,667	35,065	40,021	43,976	46,200	45,803	46,080	28,400

Question

Set up a strategy to ensure future growth of the company.

CAGES, INC.
Institutional Product Market

Mr. Russ Buchan, is the owner/manager of an established company, Cages, Inc., located in Harrisburg, Pennsylvania. The company primarily produces stainless steel animal cages and complimentary products. Besides the stainless steel cages, Mr. Buchan also produces galvanized cages. Sales of the latter amount to half those of stainless steel cages.

Buyers of Buchan's products consist of governmental, educational, and industrial facilities. Government facilities basically include federal- and state-owned research laboratories. Purchasing of animal cages by government facilities is accomplished through bid proposals and negotiations with competitors whose products meet the specifications.

Colleges, universities, and high schools make up the educational animal cage market. Breakdown of college and university sales by departments show that psychology, sociology, physics, chemistry, and biology are the primary users of animal cages. Purchasing the animal cages is usually taken care of through the central purchasing office of the institution. Also, departments may submit orders directly to the companies if the dollar value of the order is kept under a certain limit set down by the institution.

Industrial facilities which use animal cages are basically pharmaceutical companies and research facilities. Industrial facilities use animals in their research for their own products and also in contracting their research facilities out to other companies.

Submitted by David C. Low, Sales, Centex Homes Corporation, and James Maurer, Millwright

The management of Cages, Inc., consists of a purchasing agent and two plant managers. No salespeople are employed to sell the cages. Advertisements in trade magazines and catalogues are the only form of promotion used by Buchan. Mr. Buchan feels that his personal contact by telephone with his customers is the most efficient means to sell his products.

Total animal cage manufacturing sales for the industry have declined 35 percent from last year's. Cages, Inc. suffered a 30 percent decline in sales as compared to last year.

Emphasis has been placed on producing stainless steel animal cages instead of galvanized cages because the higher contribution to profits of this production operation. Market demand for stainless steel cages is also greater than that for galvanized. Research facilities basically work on long-term projects where the stainless steel cages hold up better under constant use and cleaning.

The retail market (pet shops, etc.) predominantly buys from Japanese manufacturers. Retail consumers use animal cages for short-term purposes. Buchan feels it would be unprofitable to change production facilities and produce animal cages for this retail market. He feels that high sales at a low cost would not be feasible for his operation.

Buchan had a market survey conducted to help him in his decision making. For this study, data was accumulated from personal interviews with governmental, educational, and industrial facility operators. He noticed from the survey that the majority of buyers interviewed would prefer to order from a cage manufacturer who has a salesperson call on them rather than just receiving catalogues through the mail.

Another aspect of the survey that Mr. Buchan took interest in was the decline in purchases in the three markets. Better cleaning devices and sterilization equipment and also a decrease in research grants awarded had caused an overabundance of animal cages carried as inventory.

One alternative to selling animal cages presented in detail in the report was the production of a cleaning device for animal cages. A major problem brought out by most of the interviewees was that of finding a quick and efficient way to clean their cages. Some of the larger research facilities spent thousands of dollars acquiring huge cleaning machines to wash and sterilize the cages. Many of the smaller facilities are still using manual labor for this chore. Hand cleaning is both time-consuming and inefficient.

A cleaning device is described in the report which is nothing more than a shower stall with two brackets inside to hold the cages up. Two high-pressure nozzles attached to hoses are set up for spraying water and germicide. The unit is portable and can be moved from one place to another.

In the course of the investigations, people from several cage-using facilities in the United States were interviewed. One of the establishments visited was the Swan Lake Research Center in Missouri. Swan Lake is a Department of Natural Resources field-research unit. The director of the center is Dr. Mark Borg, Head Biologist. Dr. Borg indicates that the center had little need for additional cages for animals, with one exception — the small-mammal live trap, or "treadle trap."

Dr. Borg indicated that Swan Lake would be interested in purchasing more traps of this type. He stated that this type of live trap was the best the Missouri Department of Natural Resources had, but the traps that they were using had been constructed some thirty years ago by convict labor. The cost of each trap was estimated at $8 per unit based on cost figures in the 1930s.

Dr. Borg said if he could obtain more of these traps at a reasonable price he would gladly purchase some. He indicated that there were several types of small-mammal live traps available on the market, but not one of the available traps performed as well as the treadle trap. Dr. Borg indicated that he would be willing to purchase a cage made of metal or wood, provided that it performed as well as the treadle trap. However, he did say that these traps worked better after the wood aged. He felt that the gloss or shine of the newer cages tended to scare the animals away.

The Department of Natural Resources in Missouri used these mammal traps for a variety of purposes. State and local law enforcement agencies also used them to trap pest animals. As of this date, no study has been made of other possible marketing areas for these traps, but evidence seems to indicate a wide market.

This type of product could be appealing to ecology-minded groups also. Efforts should be made to determine what amount of influence these groups have over users of such products or on future legislation in this area. Ecology groups may be able to offer help, inadvertently or through direct endorsement, in selling this product in various ways.

Questions

Where is Cages' market?

THE SEVEN BROTHERS CORPORATION (B)
Market Identification

The Seven Brothers Corporation was one of the medium-sized manufacturers of sailboats in the United States with its head-quarters in Los Angeles, California. The company president, Jim Morgan, had agreed to execute the proposed diversification of company business into pinpool as suggested by his resourceful marketing manager, Mr. Jack Robinson. A pinpool is a table that can be used for both ping pong and pool with specially designed parts. In an executive meeting, to pursue this matter further, the president was furnished with the following information submitted by his fellow executives:

Existing maximum production capacity for pinpool	20,000 units
Break-even units with promotion budget constraints of $20,000 for pinpool	13,900 units
Optimal allocation of promotional efforts with sales-person hours constraint of 5,000 hours and budget of $20,000: Sales presentation	166 times
Trade journal advertising	66 times
Optimal profit resulting from first-year pinpool operation	$24,060

Since pinpool was the first venture of its kind, the president had indicated that the company was inclined to increase its production capacity more than the present capacity made available by uti-lizing the old sailboat building plant and the suggested new in-vestment in some basic tools and machines. The best thing for the company under such a circumstance is, according to Mr. Robin-

Submitted by Dr. Kung-Mo Kuo, Assistant Professor of Business Organization and Management, The University of Wisconsin—Platteville

son, the marketing manager, to increase the budget for promotion programs and keep the production running at maximum capacity; for Mr. Robinson believed that the company could sell what could be produced at maximum capacity.

In order to assure the existence of the pinpool market, Mr. Robinson advised his researchers to conduct a survey in the state of California, the company's home state. The result of such a survey was summarized in Exhibit 5.

Exhibit 5   *Result of buyer's intention survey for Seven Brother's Pinpool, all metropolitan areas, California*

Family classification	Buyers' intention A = Interested B = Will consider C = Not interested	% distribution of buyers' intention by family classification at income level of:			
		Less than $8,000	$8,000– 14,999	More than $15,000	TOTAL
With ping pong table	A	0.00	0.00	0.00	0.00
	B	0.00	0.01	0.00	0.01
	C	0.01	7.18	91.80	99.99
	TOTAL	1.01	7.19	91.80	100.00
Pool table	A	0.00	0.00	0.00	0.00
	B	0.00	0.00	0.00	0.00
	C	0.00	1.89	98.11	100.00
	TOTAL	0.00	1.89	98.11	100.00
Without ping pong table and pool table and with 1 member	A	0.00	0.00	0.00	0.00
	B	0.00	0.01	0.00	0.01
	C	40.50	38.93	20.56	99.99
	TOTAL	40.50	38.94	20.56	100.00
Without ping pong table and pool table and with 2 members	A	0.00	0.01	0.00	0.01
	B	0.01	0.02	0.00	0.03
	C	42.10	38.50	19.36	99.96
	TOTAL	42.11	38.53	19.36	100.00
Without ping pong table and pool table and with 3 members	A	0.00	0.02	0.00	0.02
	B	0.01	0.03	0.01	0.05
	C	33.30	41.14	25.49	99.93
	TOTAL	33.31	41.19	25.50	100.00
Without ping pong table and pool table and with 4 members	A	0.01	0.03	0.00	0.04
	B	0.02	0.05	0.00	0.07
	C	38.10	39.71	22.18	99.89
	TOTAL	38.13	39.79	22.18	100.00

With information from "Households Distribution by Cash Income Groups" and "Number of Persons Per Household — Metropolitan Area of California," state total data from the 1973 edition of *Survey of Buying Power (Sales Management Magazine,* July, 1973, C11.15), and data from the population census, Mr. Robinson concluded that the sales in California alone could reach well beyond the number of units that the existing production capacity could handle.

After intensive discussion with Mr. Robinson and the company's finance manager, Ms. Sarah Victor, the president had decided to increase the budget for the promotion program. The new budget was to increase from $20,000 to $100,000. With the new budget, the company total salesperson hours for pinpool could expand from 5,000 hours to 25,000 hours.

Having the new budget made available for promotional programs, the estimated direct sales cost, administrative cost, and other costs for the pinpool operation were:

Depreciation for new tools	$ 20,000
Depreciation for building	$250,000
Administrative salaries, direct sales expenses* and other overhead costs	$227,000
Variable expenses (labor, materials, etc.)	$ 50 per pinpool machine

*All salespeople were on straight salary.

The original estimation of costs and hours involving the promotion program remained unchanged. They were:

20 hours needed for each sales presentation
25 hours needed for each ad insertion
$100 costs for each sales presentation
$50 costs for each ad insertion

Also, the profit and sales promotion relationship found by the company researchers from their study of medium-sized firms with conditions similar to Seven Brothers was considered to hold. This relationship was interpreted by the following equation:

$P = \$100S + \$80A$ (with coefficient of correlation of 0.955)

where: P = Profit before taxes
S = Sales presentation
A = Ad insertion in *Sports Illustrated*

With the new budget expansion, it was determined that the optimal profit could reach as much as $103,000 from pinpool operation the first year of operation with the production running at near-maximum capacity.

The "go" signal was finally on for the production of pinpool which was to be branded as LUCKY-7 Pinpool. While the production activities were being smoothly carried out under the direction of production manager, Tom Holfill, the marketing department was busily engaged in the preparation of promotional programs. The first order of business was, of course, to define the market, to be specific, to identify the target market, and then to determine the market potential for each geographical subunit — sales allocation. The pinpool was scheduled to be on the market by February 1, 1976.

The market was defined as California households with three and four persons per household having annual total income of between $8,000 and $14,999. The geographical subunit for sales analysis was the metropolitan areas.

If you were the executive officer of the Seven Brothers Corporation, you would have made the following decisions:

1. The existence of pinpool market
2. The budget expansion for promotion programs
3. Target market
4. Market allocation

Questions

How did you make these decisions? How are these decisions justified?

chapter

_____ 5

People and
Marketing Cases

BRANT UNIVERSITY

In recent years the Brant University yearbook has experienced steadily decreasing sales (Exhibit 1) along with decreased sub-

Exhibit 1   *Brant University's yearbook sales for the last ten years*

	Units sold or distributed
1961	7,070
1962	7,013
1963	6,688
1964	6,403
1965	5,216
1966	4,766
1967	4,250
1968	3,350
1969	3,200
1970	2,900

sidies from the university (Exhibit 2). In the past, Brant University heavily subsidized the yearbook, with the result that costs were not

Exhibit 2   *Brant University's Yearbook costs for the last ten years (printing)*

1961	$33,905
1962	28,034
1963	24,876
1964	21,003
1965	17,099
1966	15,889
1967	14,933
1968	13,867
1969	13,437
1970	12,000

Submitted by Lawrence Doody, Manager, Robert Hall Clothes, Inkster, Michigan

too closely watched; the yearbook traditionally averaged a 6–10 percent rise yearly (Exhibit 3). Under the most recent policy, the

Exhibit 3   *Brant University student enrollment*

1961	10,453
1962	10,657
1963	10,879
1964	12,011
1965	13,827
1966	14,332
1967	18,875
1968	19,832
1969	21,500
1970	22,400

university provided office space and salaries for several editors and the business manager. The university also assigned an administrator to the yearbook who acted totally as an advisor. This administrator had no decision-making power.

In 1970, the yearbook suffered a $10,000 loss. The university paid the bills and this loss was owed directly to the university. Also in 1970, Jill Atchens, Business Manager, had attended a conference of the nation's college yearbook editors. The general consensus of this conference was that in the next three to four years, many yearbooks across the country would go out of business. The majority of the editors felt that the predicted low sales was due to student apathy towards yearbooks. They argued that changing attitudes and trends among students were making the tradition-bound yearbook an unsaleable product.

The convention participants noted a few very successful yearbooks in operation at the time, but attributed their success to a campus attitude that was drastically different than the national average. They, in effect, argued that these successful yearbooks were on campuses which had not awakened to the "youth revolution." They said that these areas were actually a little slow in undergoing the changes occurring at most of the schools and that they would very shortly be experiencing the same problems as the majority of schools.

On September 12, 1971, Atchens met with the staff to start organization of the 1971–72 yearbook, and to see whether she and her staff could formulate a plan to raise sales in the forthcoming year(s). Opinion at the meeting was sharply divided into two factions. One group, led by Mr. Frank Yearing, Feature Editor, felt that the whole traditional approach of the yearbook should be scrapped. He stated that the yearbook should change its whole structure and aim its content at subjects which were relevant to the students — for example, pollution and the Vietnam War. He felt that the usual portfolio of sports, fraternity, and graduation pictures was totally inadequate in making a yearbook the students would buy.

The other group, represented chiefly by Mr. Art Duncan, Sports Editor, felt that this approach was too drastic. They pointed out that previous surveys (which had been done in 1964–65) among the student population of Brant University showed that students bought a yearbook for one of two reasons: the student's picture was in the yearbook or the student was associated with a group or organization whose picture was in the yearbook. They felt that a simple reorganization of the existing yearbook layout would suffice to raise sales. They suggested producing a plan to rearrange the coverage of various sections of the yearbook and to add more color pages. They felt that the students liked color pages better, even though the cost was about twice that of black and white.

Mr. Yearing then went on to say that he felt that the present advertising and promotional strategies were antiquated and ineffective. He felt that new techniques and methods of advertising could raise sales. Mr. Duncan replied that the present methods were all free, mainly through the campus radio station and the campus paper. He did agree with Duncan's group that the advertisement layout could stand some updating.

Mr. Yearing supported his contention of student apathy towards traditionalism on campus by citing the lack of floats at last year's Homecoming Parade and the donation of the money usually spent on the floats to charities. Moreover, he cited the high sales volume of the campus underground newspaper, *Pinko Funnies,* as evidence that students would buy material relevant to them. *Pinko Funnies* dealt with the issues brought to the forefront of public consciousness by the so-called "youth revolution." Mr. Yearing said that he felt that students thought there were many much more important issues than who is elected Homecoming Queen or who is fraternity president. Furthermore, the shifting of emphasis among the traditional sections of the yearbook during the last three years and the resultant sales figures showed that a simple reorganization would not work.

The yearbook has been printed since 1906 and until 1967 it was distributed free to all students on campus. Beginning in 1968, a fee of $1 per book was charged; in 1969 and 1970 the charge was $3; and in 1971 the cost per book was $7. The tentative price for the 1972 yearbook was set at $8.

The yearbook has a variety of expenses and means of collecting revenues. Expenses include printing costs of over $20,000 per year along with advertising costs, payroll costs, and other expenses that total over $46,000 per year. Revenue is acquired through four different methods: sales of yearbooks, which last year amounted to approximately $17,500; revenue from senior pictures (in 1971, 1600 out of 4800 seniors paid a sitting fee to have their picture taken; in addition to this fee the photography studio paid $2.50 to the yearbook for each picture); page contracts (each year various organizations pay $50 per half page to have their organization represented in the yearbook); and subsidies from the administration at Brant. Before 1967, the yearbook was receiving about $25,000 a year in allotments from the university. In 1968, the Business Manager of the yearbook, James Rankin, decided that the yearbook no longer needed this subsidy. From that year on, the money coming from the university was gradually decreased from $26,700 in 1968 to $3,000 in 1971.

Important considerations regarding the problems confronting the yearbook staff were:

1. The yearbook market was segmented. It was divided by class: seniors, juniors, etc. It was also, in the past, assumed to be segmented into groups or organizations. This was significant because the majority of the students who bought yearbooks were either seniors or members of an organization, buying the yearbook for their pictures. However, these assumptions had a significance which was overlooked. The yearbook was selling to only a very small portion of their potential market, and the staff made a false conclusion about the reasons for which students bought yearbooks. This caused them to concentrate the yearbook on groups and graduating seniors and fail to include anything in the yearbook to attract the vast majority of students who did not fit into these two categories.

2. The underground newspaper sales figures were rather vague; they were just called "high" in Mr. Yearing's talk with the editor.

3. In the matter of content, the comparison between the underground newspaper and the yearbook was significant. The material that was in the underground newspaper was exactly what Mr. Yearing wanted to concentrate on in the yearbook. However, a sales volume discussion may not be completely analogous. The yearbook sold for $8 and the paper sold for $.50.

4. According the university officials, the administration could no longer afford to subsidize the yearbook as it did before 1967, with all other university costs rising.

5. Each year less than half of all seniors have their pictures taken and placed in the yearbook. Every year there is an advertising

campaign to get seniors to pose for pictures. This includes advertisements in the university student newspaper and announcements on the student-run FM radio station. The response has been fairly good, but still far below expected levels.

6. Every organization and dormitory on campus is sent a contract and 95 percent of these return the contracts, buying pages in the yearbook.

7. Since 1968, there has been no advertising in the yearbook. Before that, local merchants bought space and advertisements were placed in the yearbook. In 1968, it was decided that the ads in the back of the book detracted from the quality of the book and they were eliminated.

8. The average price of yearbooks across the country is between $9 and $10. Thus, Brant's price is below comparable books across the country.

Questions

What has caused the decline of yearbook sales?

Who are yearbook purchasers?

Define a product (yearbook) and strategy which will obtain the maximum yearbook sales possible at Brant.

CRISTOFF'S DEPARTMENT STORE

Cristoff's, a large fashion retailer in the Los Angeles area, was seeking to determine why its sales were down generally and specifically during the last July sweater promotion. (This promotion had usually been one in which the stores enjoyed high sales.)

Mr. Johnson, an executive of the company, interviewed Mr. Finneren, manager of the Anaheim Mall store. Mr. Finneren said that it was often necessary to make numerous phone calls to other stores to transfer merchandise which his store lacked or which was not sent out in sufficient quantities from the warehouse. Mr. Finneren said further that it was not unusual to find the store where he located the item either having a surplus of that particular size or style or a shortage in an item of which Anaheim had an excess.

During the next month, Mr. Johnson inspected three Cristoff's stores attempting to evaluate why there was an excess of "dogs" and an insufficient number of "hot items." Mr. Johnson first visited the West Grand Boulevard stores, then the Santa Monica shopping center store, and the downtown area.

Mr. Johnson arrived just before lunch hour at the West Grand Boulevard store. The store, ranked fifth in sales, is located in the downtown area across from a building which houses several hundred offices. Johnson spoke to Mary Wellington, the assistant manager. Wellington said that they too were having problems getting the correct merchandise into the West Grand store.

Mr. Johnson remained at the store until after the employee lunch hours, noting that the average customer was female, approximately forty years of age, black, with portly physical character-

Submitted by Marie Ziomek Johnson

istics. Many women came in during their lunch hours from the office building across the street wanting large-size (misses) sweaters for their air-conditioned offices, not the junior-size turtlenecks shipped to Cristoff's for the past July sweater promotion. Mr. Johnson noted a shortage of salespeople during the busy lunch hours.

The next week, Mr. Johnson visited the store located in the Santa Monica shopping center. The customers appeared to be in the upper-middle income group, approximately thirty to thirty-five years of age. Their busiest time (according to Mr. Smith, store manager) was between 1 P.M. and 4 P.M., after the lunch hour and before dinner.

The store personnel consisted of high school co-op students; since, Mr. Smith said, there were few more mature women in the surrounding area who needed to work. Mr. Johnson noted that the store had an overage of large-size cardigans. There was also a shortage of washable pantsuits which are popular for younger, more active housewives. Mr. Smith commented that he was always "almost out" of junior sizes in the sportswear department.

The third week of investigation Mr. Johnson arrived at the five-floor downtown store, which is ranked first in sales in the chain. He observed that the store had an almost entirely black clientele. The merchandise was extremely well-suited to the customers and emphasized the high fashion Afro-American fashions. The downtown store was very active on the particular Friday afternoon. The black store manager, Miss Killian, said that Mr. Johnson had arrived at a most opportune time. The lunch hours (11:30 A.M. to 1:30 P.M.) are the most hectic part of the day and Miss Killian attempts to stagger breaks and lunch hours for the salespeople to allow adequate floor coverage. Mr. Johnson found this store's greatest need to be in small junior sizes and large-size pantsuits.

At the end of his inspection, Mr. Johnson attempted to evaluate how Cristoff's could determine what merchandise should go to each store. Further examination revealed that:

1. There are fifty stores in the chain which spread over the three states of California, Washington, and Oregon.
2. The sales of Cristoff's, Inc., in 1975 was $55,000,000.
3. Mr. Johnson interviewed the managers and assistant managers during the month of August, directly after the July sales decrease was noticed.
4. It was felt that, upon inspection of the four stores mentioned, a good cross-sectional view was gained concerning Cristoff's clothing operation.

More specifically, the four particular stores examined had the following characteristics:

1. *Anaheim:* This store was a product of the big "suburban move" by retailers to serve better the thousands of people moving out of the city. Since many stores have been built by Cristoff's for this reason, the Anaheim store gives a fair indication of the conditions existing in the others.
2. *Santa Monica:* Mostly upper-class people live in the vicinity of this store and thus it introduces a high-quality taste clientele store into the sample.
3. *West Grand Boulevard:* This store was included in the sample because it had the highest amount of traffic of any Cristoff's store.
4. *Downtown Store:* The downtown store is indeed a special case and thus examination of other stores could not serve as a predictor of what goes on downtown. This store is not only the largest in the Cristoff's chain, but it is heavily frequented by blacks. Further, since the 1967 riots, the percentage of white customers has been on the decrease. Consequently, since the clientele composition and volume of customers has been constantly changing, this store must be examined specifically, as the traits of no other store can serve to predict what would be the best policy for this store.
5. During 1975, it was reported that two stores were operating at a loss. During the last half of the year, both of the stores closed. "Both stores were located in neighborhoods with specialized clientele," as was reported by Cristoff's top management. One store was situated in Beverly Hills, a most affluent and infuential city. Most women in this community preferred high-fashion couturier designs found at the exclusive shops. The other store was located in an area with a large Jewish population, where strong ethnic ties compelled the women to patronize Jewish proprietors.
6. Due to Cristoff's strong central management, there is no opportunity for individualizing each store's position in the community.

Questions

How does Cristoff's take into consideration the difference in life styles, peer groups, consumer motivation, and behavior differences in general of the markets in which its stores are located?

EBREW'S SPORTING GOODS COMPANY

Ebrew's Sporting Goods Company manufactures fishing equipment such as rods, reels, line, and assorted fishing tackle. Ebrew's is located in Minneapolis, Minnesota, and markets its products mainly in northern Minnesota. In Minneapolis and the immediate vicinity, Ebrew's markets directly to retailers by way of its own trucks; but, in the outlying northern areas, sporting goods distributors are used to reach the retail outlets. The main retail outlets are department stores, sporting goods stores, and discount department stores, with smaller amounts of sales going to drug stores and hardware stores.

The two main distributors used are Wao Distributors and Sportco Distributors. Wao Distributors cater to mass merchandisers — mainly discount and chain stores — with a limited amount of business going to independents. Sportco Distributors deal exclusively with retail sporting goods stores. These distributors handle many different models and makes. The main services the distributors provide the manufacturer and retailer are handling defective merchandise, setting up store displays, providing the retailer with promotional material supplied by the manufacturer, storage of inventory, writing orders, and meeting retailers' merchandising needs.

Ebrew's Sporting Goods Company was established in 1950 by Gerald Ebrew and James Brock as a manufacturer of quality fishing equipment. For about twenty years, Ebrew's was thought of by fishermen as the best producer of quality rods, reels, line, and assorted fishing tackle.

Submitted by Dell James Brokaw, General Motors — Oldsmobile Division

Exhibit 4   *Sales in southwestern Minnesota market*
              (in thousands of dollars)

	1950	1955	1960	1965	1968	1969	1970	1971	1972	1973	1974	1975
Smith:												
Rods	2	4	8	11	16	21	24	30	34	42	43	48
Reels	4	5	9	13	18	23	27	33	37	46	55	62
Line	1	2	3	3	4	5	6	7	8	9	9	9
Tackle	3	3	5	8	12	16	18	23	26	31	35	41
TOTAL	10	14	25	35	50	65	75	93	105	128	142	160
Sunset:												
Rods	1	2	5	9	13	19	24	31	35	40	42	45
Reels	2	3	6	10	14	20	25	32	36	45	53	64
Line	1	1	2	3	4	5	6	7	8	9	10	11
Tackle	1	2	5	8	11	15	19	25	29	36	40	42
TOTAL	5	8	18	30	42	59	74	95	108	130	145	162
Holliday:												
Rods	2	3	6	10	13	16	22	29	33	36	39	43
Reels	2	3	6	11	15	19	25	32	36	40	44	49
Line	1	1	2	3	4	5	6	7	7	7	7	8
Tackle	1	2	5	8	13	15	20	26	29	32	35	38
TOTAL	6	9	19	32	45	55	73	94	105	115	125	138
Ebrews:												
Rods	3	5	7	10	13	18	20	24	30	36	41	47
Reels	4	5	8	13	16	21	23	27	32	38	44	50
Line	1	1	3	5	7	8	8	9	9	9	9	9
Tackle	3	3	7	9	12	16	17	20	24	29	34	39
TOTAL	11	14	25	37	48	63	68	80	95	112	128	145

In 1968, one of three manufacturers who had been mainly concerned with low- and middle-priced fishing equipment decided to enter the quality fishing equipment market. This competing manufacturer, Smith Sporting Goods Company, established itself with a wide variety of models of rods, spinning and spin-casting reels, different pound test lines, and assorted fishing tackle. The resultant competition between the two companies did not decrease Ebrew's share of the fishing equipment market, because the total fishing equipment market increased substantially. In 1970, however, the other two manufacturers (Sunset Company and Holliday Company) established themselves in the fishing equipment market with a wide variety of prices and quality in rods and reels and a wide assortment of pound test lines and other fishing tackle. Exhibit 4 shows the sales of Ebrew's and its competitors from 1950 to 1975.

Ebrew's competitors entered the high-quality fishing equipment market with up-to-date features not incorporated into Ebrew's fishing equipment. In 1972, Ebrew's increased its number of models of rods and reels and varieties of pound test lines, and assorted fishing tackle in order to meet the competition in the ever-popular fishing gear market. Sunset Company and Smith Company both decided in 1973 to come out with top of the line deluxe spin-casting reels with new features and a price tag of about $25.00 retail.

In 1974, Mr. Robert White, sales manager for Ebrew's Sporting Goods Company, was contemplating competing with Sunset and Smith Companies for the deluxe spin-casting reel market, but he did not know what consumer and retailer reactions would be. He knew that his company accounted for a fairly large percentage of discount department store fishing equipment sales. In sporting goods stores and department stores, Ebrew's percentage of the fishing equipment market had slipped somewhat since 1973.

Exhibit 5   *Percentage of sales per manufacturer*

Discount department stores:	1970	1971	1972	1973	1974	1975
Sunset	21	20	21	23	23	23
Smith	26	26	25	25	24	23
Holliday	23	24	23	18	18	18
Ebrew's	26	26	28	30	31	32
Others	4	4	2	4	4	4
TOTAL	100	100	100	100	100	100
Department stores:						
Sunset	14	20	20	25	27	28
Smith	30	25	24	27	28	28
Holliday	18	21	20	18	17	18
Ebrew's	32	29	30	24	22	20
Others	6	5	6	6	6	6
TOTAL	100	100	100	100	100	100
Sporting goods stores:						
Sunset	16	20	21	26	28	29
Smith	29	25	24	27	27	28
Holliday	19	24	23	17	18	18
Ebrew's	31	26	27	23	20	18
Others	5	5	5	7	7	7
TOTAL	100	100	100	100	100	100

Retailers relied mostly on national advertising, cooperative advertising, and personal selling by salespeople to promote their fishing equipment. National advertising was paid for by manufacturers and consisted mainly of advertising placed in sports magazines. Cooperative advertising — usually through a local newspaper or on television — included rebates and discounts on merchandise bought in large quantities. The manufacturers promote their fishing equipment using mostly the same media, cooperative advertising, and personal selling through informational booklets describing the product.

At the present time, Mr. White is studying the results of research done by Brewer and Associates into the fishing reel market. He is still trying to make up his mind on what to recommend to the president concerning the idea of going into the deluxe spin-casting reel market to compete with Sunset and Smith. Brewer and Associates distributed (some personally and some by mail) about 200 questionnaires to retailers and 200 different questionnaires to fishermen randomly scattered throughout northern Minnesota. With a response of 50 percent of the questionnaires, the 100 retailers who handled fishing equipment and the 100 fishermen who responded were analyzed.

The retailer questionnaires contained eight questions. The questions and percentage responses are listed below:

1. What is the best spin-casting reel you carry?
   Response:

Sunset	29%
Smith	31%
Ebrew's	15%
Holliday	14%
Other	11%

2. Do you feel it is worthwhile carrying high-priced spin-casting reels?
   Response:

Yes	82%
No	8%

3. What estimated percentage of sales does your best spin-casting reel have out of all your reels sold?
   Response:

Percentage of retailers:	Percentage of market for spin-casting reels:
2%	6–10%
10%	11–15%
13%	16–20%
15%	21–25%
30%	26–30%
17%	31–35%
9%	36–40%
4%	41–50%

4. Do you run any type of special promotion to sell your best spin-casting reel?
   Response:

Yes	12%
No	88%

5. Do you have available any type of promotional aid from the manufacturer of the reel?
   Response:

Yes	93%
No	7%

6. Please rank the features that you feel are important in selling spin-casting reels?

   Majority response: *(First is most important)*

Smoothness of operation	1
Appearance	2
Price	3
Weight	4
Size	5
Reversibility	6
Variety of test lines	7
Balance	8
Drag	9
Serviceability	10

7. Do you carry more than one brand of deluxe spin-casting reel?
   Response:

Yes	68%
No	32%

8. Do you feel there is room in the existing market for an Ebrew's deluxe spin-casting reel?
   Response:

Yes	91%
No	9%

The consumer questionnaire contained eight questions. The questions and their percentage responses are listed below:

1. How often do you fish during the fishing season?
   Response:

2 to 3 times per season	14%
1 to 2 times a month in season	27%
1 or more times a week in season	59%

2. What type of reel do you own? Manufacturer's name?
   Response:

Sunset	28%
Smith	26%
Ebrew's	19%
Holliday	18%
Other	9%

3. Please rank the following features that you feel are important in purchasing your reel.

   Majority response: *(First is most important)*

Smoothness of operation	1
Appearance	2
Drag	3
Price	4
Balance	5
Serviceability	6
Size	7
Variety of test lines	8
Weight	9
Reversibility	10

4. Did you hear about your reel by word of mouth or from one of the
   advertising media?
   Response:

Media advertising	76%
Word of mouth	24%

5. From what advertising media did you hear about your fishing reel?
   Response:

Radio	0%
Television	5%
Newspapers	17%
Magazines	54%
Others	24%

6. What type of retail outlet sold you your reel?
   Response:

Drug store	0%
Hardware store	6%
Department store	19%
Discount department store	39%
Sporting goods store	31%
Other	5%

7. How much would you spend for a deluxe spin-casting reel?
   Response:

$10 – 12	1%	$31 – 35	17%
$13 – 15	2%	$36 – 40	8%
$16 – 20	10%	$41 – 50	2%
$21 – 25	27%	Over $50	1%
$26 – 30	32%		

8. Would you buy an Ebrew's deluxe spin-casting reel if it were available?
   Response:

Yes	75%
No	25%

Questions
for Consideration

1. Should Ebrew's produce a deluxe top-of-the-line spin-casting reel?
2. What features should be stressed in selling a new deluxe spin-casting reel?
3. What retail price range should the new reel include?
4. What sales promotion is necessary to market effectively a new deluxe spin-casting reel?
5. What retail outlets should be emphasized in selling a new deluxe reel?
6. What type of person would buy the new deluxe reel?
7. What are the weaknesses of the competitors in the spin-casting reel market?
8. How can Ebrew's take advantage of the weaknesses of the competition?
9. What channels of distribution should be used to market the new reel?

Brewer and Associates believe:

1. Ebrew's should produce a deluxe top-of-the-line spin-casting reel to compete with Smith Company and Sunset Company because of the responses to the retailer and consumer questionnaire, expansion in the total fishing equipment market, and the sagging Ebrew sales in the department stores and sporting goods stores. Retailers feel it is worthwhile carrying high-priced spin-casting reels; these reels comprise a significant part of the fishing reel market; and retailers usually carry more than one brand of deluxe spin-casting reel. Retailers also feel

there is room for Ebrew's in the existing spin-casting reel market. Consumers own more Sunset and Smith reels than Ebrew's reels, according to the survey, and a consumer majority said they would buy an Ebrew's deluxe spin-casting reel if one was available.

2. The features that should be stressed in selling a new spin-casting reel should be smoothness of operation, appearance, price, and balance acording to consumer and retailer ranking of important features. These features are what the consumer feels are important. Therefore retailers must stress them and Ebrew's include them in the product to sell a new deluxe spin-casting reel effectively.

3. The price range that should be included should be between $21 to $30, because that is a price 59 percent of the consumers said they would spend for a deluxe spin-casting reel, and $25 is about the price Sunset Company and Smith Company set for their deluxe spin-casting reels.

4. The sales promotion that is necessary to market a new deluxe spin casting reel effectively must include national magazine advertisements, local newspaper advertisements on a co-operative basis, point-of-purchase displays, and pamphlets, both to aid salespeople and to distribute to the public. Advertisements tend to inform fishermen more than word of mouth and the salesperson must be able to demonstrate the product to sell it. The above promotions must be included to market the new deluxe spin-casting reel.

5. The retail outlets that should be emphasized in selling a new deluxe reel should be department stores, sporting goods stores, and discount department stores with special emphasis on department stores and sporting goods stores, since sales are lagging in these stores without a quality spin-casting reel to compete with Sunset Company and Smith Company. The largest percentage of reels were bought in discount department stores according to consumer response on the questionnaire. The three types of stores accounted for close to 90 percent of retail outlets where the sample purchased their reels.

6. The type of person that would be most likely to buy the new deluxe spin-casting reel would be the person who fishes one or more times a week during fishing season, according to the consumer survey (59 percent), and would be willing to spend $21 to $30 (59 percent) for a deluxe spin-casting reel. This person would enjoy fishing and enjoy the status of a high-priced reel.

7. The main weaknesses of the competitors' promotional strategy in the spin-casting reel market are the low usage of newspapers and inadequate special promotions, as indicated by the responses to the consumer and retailer questionnaires.
8. Ebrew's can take advantage of the weaknesses in the competitions' strategies by the cooperative usage of newspapers and by having special fishing clinics during fishing season to push the new deluxe spin-casting reel along with the rest of the products. A special introductory offer with a special low price to introduce the new reel to the fishermen should be included along with films about well-known fishermen and well-known fishing spots to get fishermen into the stores and acquainted with Ebrew's merchandise.
9. The channels of distribution that should be used are the same channels used for the other lower-priced reels. Wao Distributors and Sportco Distributors should be used with a mark-up sufficient to make them push the deluxe reel and supply the excellent services they have been supplying the retailer and manufacturer. The discount department store, department store, and sporting goods store should be emphasized, as mentioned before.

Questions

Do you think a sufficient number of retailers and consumers would purchase a high-quality priced spin-casting reel? Why? If you answered yes to the question above, how should Ebrew's market the product?

HASSON'S

On September 12, 1976, Mr. Albert Sinclair, the Vice-President and General Manager of Hasson's Menswear, was returning home from a late meeting with his branch store managers and assistant managers. Some staffing difficulties, of which he had been aware for some time, seemed to be coming to a head. They took up an increasing amount of time at each management meeting and in fact had tonight occupied the majority of their time. Regardless of how serious the situation actually was, the important thing was that his managers felt it was serious.

Hasson's Menswear first opened its doors in downtown Austin, Texas, in 1939. The proprietor was Hasson Gallop. Mr. Gallop continued to operate his modestly successful haberdashery until early in 1957. At that time, a development in the retail business brought hard times to Hasson's. Larger clothing stores began to move into Austin, along with several department stores sporting large men's clothing departments. All of these haberdasheries were backed with large amounts of capital. This capital support enabled them to carry large inventories and institute a new set of credit terms — thirty days same as cash. In other words, no interest was charged on credit sales paid for within thirty days of purchase.

Hasson Gallop simply did not have enough capital to compete in these areas. His business began to slip. In June of 1951, Gallop received what he considered a reasonable offer for the business, from one of his competitors, Sam Cohen.

Submitted by Tim L. McPartlin, Account Executive, Batten, Barton, Durstine and Osborn, Inc., Dallas, Texas

Cohen had a menswear store about four blocks from Gallop's in downtown Austin. Cohen also had a considerable amount of backup capital and was looking for an avenue of expansion. Then, as now, the public attitudes toward Jewish merchants were not always the most desirable customer attitudes. Cohen's store was widely known to be a Jewish concern. For this reason Cohen was looking for another store with a different type of image, into which he could funnel some of his available capital, and possibly expand in the future. Hasson's looked like the right store.

In late 1957, Cohen bought 100 percent of the stock of the newly incorporated Hasson's Menswear. In the sales agreement, Cohen agreed to retain Gallop at a comfortable salary until the latter voluntarily retired, or until his death. In consideration Cohen got the right to retain the use of Hasson Gallop's name and trademarks.

With the increased capital pumped in by Sam Cohen, Hasson's was once more back in the competition. The store was expanded, the inventory increased, and the new credit terms were thirty days same as cash.

Early in 1962, Cohen purchased a larger three-story building on Austin's main street. Later that year, he moved the expanded Hasson's to this location. Business was good.

In 1964, a branch store of Hasson's was opened by Cohen on the outskirts of Austin in a small shopping center. This store, called Hasson's Town and Country, was an immediate success. In its second year of operation, it surpassed the downtown store in sales.

Around this time, the downtown Austin area — as a shopping area — began to decline, stores closed, and businesses moved out to suburban shopping centers. Sam Cohen was aware of this decline in the downtown area; so he vigorously pursued an expansion program in other suburban areas north and east of Houston.

The next branch of Hasson's was opened in 1967 in Dallas, Texas, and the fourth store was opened in 1969 in Lubbock, Texas. Both branches were extremely successful, the Dallas branch particularly. The Dallas store pulled heavily from nearby industry.

The fifth branch of Hasson's was opened in March of 1974. It is part of a large indoor mall in San Antonio, Texas. By the end of 1975, the San Antonio store was the sales leader of the Hasson chain. There were plans in the works to open two additional branches in late 1976.

Office Staff

Each store has a credit manager. These managers have been with Hasson's for from five to thirty-one years. Each of the women, who serve as managers of their respective offices and office personnel — with the exception of one — are middle-aged and very experienced in credit work. All five are skilled managers. Due largely to the skill and diligence of these five women, the Hasson charge accounts are in very good condition. Hasson's has a large number of charge customers, the vast number of which are very good accounts. Each credit manager has a staff of office personnel, secretaries, and cashiers under her. These staffs vary from one person in the lagging downtown store to eight in San Antonio and in Dallas. (See Exhibit 6.)

Albert Sinclair asked his branch managers to begin compiling concrete data on their staffing problems. In a six-week period, the credit (office) managers came up with the data detailed in Exhibit

Exhibit 6.   *Attendance record — office staff*

	Number in office staff	Number of school-girls	Young unmarried	Over 35
Downtown	1	0	1	0
Austin—suburban	4	1	2	1
Dallas	8	4	2	2
Lubbock	5	2	3	0
San Antonio	8	5	1	2
TOTAL	26	12	9	5

		Number of school-girls	Young unmarried	Over 35
Average number of hours worked per week		36 hours	43.5 hours	31 hours
Total average hours worked per week for each category		436 hours	391.5 hours	155 hours
Average time with company		.68 years	2.2 years	7.1 years

ATTENDANCE

Average number of unexcused absences per year		7	8.5	2
Average number of sick days per year		11	10.2	5
Average number of times tardy per year		19	14	8

6. Generally, the credit managers felt that the best office help came from mature women (preferably over forty) either unmarried or with grown children. "They are more dependable, harder working, and more efficient" was a common statement. The data seems to reinforce these statements and points out the disturbing fact that, out of approximately 983 hours worked by office help, only 155 were worked by this desirable group. 828 hours were worked by the less than desirable younger women. "They make more mistakes, have less interest in their jobs, and accomplish much less in the same amount of time" was one comment made about the younger women in comparison with their elders.

Sales Staff

Similarly, the branch managers and their assistants collected data on their sales and stock personnel. Like the office staffs, the sales staffs too were plagued with young temporary help who seemed to have little genuine interest or ambition for their jobs.

The clothing (i.e. suits and topcoats) and sportswear (sportscoats and dress slacks) salespeople were not included in this "staff study." These employees were generally seasoned veterans of the "rag business," dependable professionals, with good total sales, and more important, high average sales.

The inefficiency, then, was felt to be in the shoe, young men's, and furnishings departments. Exhibit 7 is an analysis similar to the one for the office staff. The data compiled on the sales staff

Exhibit 7   *Attendance record — sales staff*

	Number in sales staff	*Number of schoolboys*	*Young unmarried*	*Married*
Downtown	4	2	2	0
Austin—suburban	16	10	2	2
Dallas	24	14	6	4
Lubbock	22	12	8	2
San Antonio	24	16	2	6
Total	90	54	20	14
Average number of hours worked per week		37 hours	44 hours	28 hours
Total average hours worked per week for each category		1998 hours	880 hours	392 hours
Average time with company		.52 years	2.9 years	9.2 years

Attendance

Average number of unexcused absences per year	10	11.4	2
Average number of sick days per year	14	13	4
Average number of times tardy per year	18	21	8

is very similar to that collected on the office staff, with one exception. The sales staff can be checked for efficiency in a more objective manner — by comparing sales records. This mass of data has been condensed into an average sale per customer for each of the three categories of salespeople:

School-age	AS/C	$11.57
Young unmarried	AS/C	$22.03
Married	AS/C	$46.23

The comments which accompanied this data paralleled that from the office managers. The young temporary help who worked the great bulk of the hours were uninterested, unmotivated, and inefficient.

But inefficiency in the sales situation was not the only personnel problem that the branch managers were concerned about. Customer complaints about curt and impolite salespeople were increasing at an alarming rate, as was internal theft and shrinkage.

Customer Relations

Sinclair also instructed his managers to gather data on customer complaints about store personnel. Every employee at every branch was required to wear an attractive, brightly colored name tag, and customers were encouraged to identify salespeople and office workers by name. Then, hopefully, when they had complaints they would register complaints by name also. Exhibit 8 shows the results of this program.

Exhibit 8   *Customer complaints about personnel*

	Office			Sales		
	School-girls	Young unmarried	Over 40	School-boys	Young unmarried	Married
Total complaints	27	31	4	117	91	24
Total number of people in each category	12	9	5	54	20	14
Average per person	2.25	3.44	.8	2.16	4.55	1.7

It must be kept in mind that a customer generally does not lodge a complaint to management about an employee unless he is very upset. So, although the average number of complaints per employee for this three-month period is small in an absolute sense, it is serious. For every one, verbally reported complaint there may be as high as fifteen or twenty incidents of irritation. It is interesting to note in this data that, although once again the older help is significantly better in this area, it is the young unmarrieds who represent the bulk of the problem, not the school-age help.

The branch managers felt that this customer relations situation was by far the most serious aspect of their staffing problem, at least over the long run. Hasson's had worked hard and spent a great deal of money to create its image as a store that really cared about its customers. They heavily advertised a competent, helpful, friendly sales staff and practiced the old retail maxim, "the customer is always right," to the letter. Hasson's was not a self-service store. The company policy was to greet every customer who entered the store with a salesman who followed through until the sale was made. This general policy helps explain the extreme concern of the branch managers about the rising tide of complaints about their salespeople.

Another problem which was serious at every branch was internal shrinkage, or employee theft. Because of the nature of theft and the complicating factor of customer theft, it was difficult to get any firm data from this area. Most of the discussion of this problem had centered around the intuitive feelings of the branch managers. However, they did agree on several points.

1. They felt that the great majority of the internal theft was directly attributable to the young employees.
2. Employees on the sales floor were stealing small items that were hard to inventory and would fit in a coat pocket, like ties, cufflinks, or socks.
3. Large items were not being taken off the sales floor.
4. Big-ticket items, however, were leaving the store from the receiving and stock departments. (All of the stockpersonnel and receiving room personnel in all branches were under twenty-one years of age).

The following comments were also agreed to by most of the managers as characterizing their store: The young salesclerks seemed to have a greater compulsion to steal items they could not afford, because it was important for them to be in style, to "look sharp." They were more concerned with style, with "what's cool," with their looks, than the older clerks. Their attitudes toward theft were often less severe. Many considered "whatever you can steal" as a kind of fringe benefit of the job.

It was not believed that salesclerks were taking big-ticket items, though. Each store was set up for maximum visibility of all sales areas and either the manager or the assistant manager was always on the floor.

The above situation is not very different from that found in most retail stores and it might have been tolerated. However, it was further felt that large numbers of big-ticket merchandise were being taken out via the receiving and stock rooms.

The situation was first brought to Sinclair's attention eighteen months earlier when an outside security consulting firm submitted their report to him, following a six-month study. The crux of the study's findings was that, although shoplifting and customer theft at Hasson's were very close to the industry average, total shrinkage was almost double the industry figures. It was the consensus of the management that this discrepancy was caused by the receiving and stock employees. These employees, it was determined, have many opportunities to conceal merchandise either on their persons or in trash boxes, outgoing mail, or deliveries, without danger of observation, and to get it easily and safely out of the store.

It was estimated by this security report that internal theft amounted to an average of between $250 to $300 for every company employee (several times the acceptable rate).

Mr. Sinclair sees several reasons why Hasson's is having a hard time getting good help. The retail business does not pay its help well: usually Hasson's scale is just $.10 to $.15 above the current minimum wage. Furthermore, the hours demanded of retail salesclerks are long: four of Hasson's five stores are open from 9:30 A.M. to 9:00 P.M. six days a week, and some Sundays in busy seasons. The combination of low pay and long hours make retail sales unattractive to mature, settled people with families to support (the most desirable group, as determined by Hasson's data).

Retailing does attract high school and college students who need a source of income, until they finish their educations and move on to their chosen fields, young single people who need a job in the interim until they can decide what they really want or find something better, and older housewives and semiretired men who enjoy having something to do and supplementing their income. All of these are rather uninterested, temporary help.

The problem is further complicated by the fact that interaction with an upper middle-class clientele necessitates that the salespeople be articulate, personable, and spend a significant amount of their small incomes on clothing and appearance. This is a tall order because of the poor pay scale in retailing.

Methods of Payment

School-age help is paid between $1.65 and $2.25 per hour plus 1 percent of their total sales at retail, paid monthly. Part-time help is usually paid an hourly amount against 6 percent of their total retail sales, adjusted monthly. Regular full-time sales help is paid a weekly salary of $125.00 against 6 percent of their total retail sales, adjusted monthly. The lack of dedicated professional people in retail sales is usually laid to this low pay scale.

Questions

What effect are these personnel problems likely to have on customer relations?

How should Hasson's solve the personnel problems?

chapter

6

Product Management Cases

K & K POWER SYSTEMS
Is There a Market: At What Price?

With the introduction of the Beatles and the music of the 1960s, the sound of a rock group became of primary importance. Much research and money went into the design of equipment which could reproduce sounds clearly and precisely at high audio output.

Of high importance was the faithful reproduction of the vocal part of the music. The purchase of a good public address system (P.A.) and, for that matter, basic guitar speakers entailed a great deal of money. Nine hundred dollars was an average figure for a combination amplifier and speaker P.A., $700 of which was the speaker system.

Mr. Kay, who owned a music store, felt that too much money went into the chrome and trim on these units. Relying on what his customers had led him to believe — that sound was important above all, and not looks — he and a friend, Mr. Kern, designed a basic, low-priced enclosure system.

The system utilized a folded-horn design and contained one of the best lifetime guaranteed speakers on the market. The enclosure was basically larger than most, but it was designed in such a way as to utilize this extra volume to produce at maximum efficiency.

Each unit was made entirely of plywood and glued together. It was flat black in color and had nothing external which could be damaged.

Submitted by Greg Nowak

Exhibit 1   *A basic enclosure system*

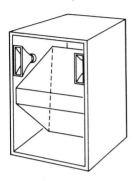

These structures were easily adapted to guitar or P.A. use by a simple speaker changeover.

The material costs for one of these systems which were built in his friend's home shop in three hours time, ran as follows:

2 5 × 7 pieces of plywood	$15.00
1 Altec Lancing speaker	65.00
2 Horn speakers	16.00
1 Crossover network	10.00
Paint and glue	1.00
Labor estimate	25.00
Total cost	$132.00

The finished product was comparable in sound and design to one brand-name speaker system which cost $450.00

After building several dozen of each type of enclosure — both P.A. and guitar — and having them used by local groups, the partners received a very favorable response. Many inquiries resulted as to price and where the units could be purchased. Mr. Kay had tentatively set the price at $250.00, and was contemplating going into production on a larger scale.

Patent rights had been applied for. Distribution through other dealers was under consideration at a cost of $180 (this would entail a 28 percent mark-up for sale to consumers at a price of $250).

Questions

Is there a market for this product? Explain. Can Kay and Kern successfully market the product? Explain.

KENLEY
Adding to a Successful Product Line

In the summer of 1976, Mr. Gar, the sole owner of the Kenley Drapery Center, was confronted with deciding whether to expand the product lines of his store to include ready-made curtains for the home. This was considered a major policy decision by Mr. Gar because of the changes needed in advertising and promotional policy. A new department would also have to be worked into the already existing floor plan of the store.

This medium-sized specialty store is located in Arlington, Texas, with an annual gross sales of $750,000. Its sales are concentrated in the metropolitan Dallas and Fort Worth areas, but some sales originate as far away as 300 miles. The average family income of those buying drapes from Kenley Drapery Center is $16,000. These customers are mainly those who are married and have settled down in homes of their own. Since the center does handle high-quality materials, the ages of these mature customers are between twenty-eight and fifty-two. Kenley also handles contract work for various home developers in the surrounding metro-

Exhibit 2   *Model home drapery contracts*

Developer	Number of models per year	Percent of total sales
MGM	50	13.0
Capital	36	10.0
Thunderbird	14	4.5
Bridgeview	10	3.5
Olympus	32	9.0
	140	40.0

Submitted by Paul Catalano

politan areas (Exhibit 2). This work includes the installation and designing of drapes in the styles and textures desired. These drapes installed in the model homes are then sold as part of the total price of the house. Contracts account for 40 percent of the entire sales of Kenley per year.

Another 40 percent of the sales per year come from the private homeowner described in Exhibit 3. The majority of these people have given as reasons for their patronage the quality of the

Exhibit 3   *Consumer expenditures*

	Metropolitan households		Expenditures for custom drapes		Expenditures for ready-made curtains	
	Number of households	Percent of households	Average $ expenditures	Percent of total market	Average $ expenditures	Percent of total market
Annual household income						
Under $12,000	8,610	18	6	5	26	16
$12,000–$12,999	7,080	14	12	8	17	21
$13,000–$13,999	7,510	15	18	13	9	22
$14,000–$14,999	9,250	19	21	18	7	16
$15,000–$16,999	9,680	20	31	29	5	11
$17,000–$19,999	4,680	9	35	16	5	9
$20,000 and over	2,330	5	52	11	2	5
Education of household head						
Grade school or less	9,380	19	13	11	5	12
Finished grade school	10,170	21	14	13	4	10
Some high school	9,080	18	22	19	7	17
Finished high school	10,860	22	26	27	8	24
Some college or beyond	9,650	20	32	30	15	37
Age of household head						
Under 30 years	6,360	13	41	25	15	25
30–39 years	12,030	24	28	32	9	29
40–49 years	10,290	21	22	22	7	20
50–64 years	12,700	26	13	15	7	22
65 years and older	7,760	16	8	6	2	4

draperies and the guarantee offered with every installation. Mr. Gar has samples from which customers make selections plus additional combinations in various booklets. He gives useful advice to all his customers in the selection of the proper rods, design, and color in relation to the style and color of their furniture.

The custom drapes are then made up by expert seamstresses and delivered and installed at the customer's specified time by Kenley's own privately trained workmen. These people work directly for Mr. Gar and, in some cases, are also his sales personnel.

Fifteen percent of the remaining 20 percent of annual sales is obtained through competitive contracts. They yield only about 2–3 percent profit on the dollar. Competitive-bid customers include professional buildings, schools, and office buildings. Finally, the last 5 percent of annual sales comes from in-store sales of rods, fixtures, and other smaller items used in drapery installation and care.

Exhibit 4   *Sales by type*

Model homes	40%
Homeowners	40
Contracts	15
Miscellaneous	5
	100%

As mentioned above, the Kenley Drapery Center has a guarantee on all drapes bought. The guarantee is that if the drapes are returned to the center for cleaning — and only to Kenley — and are damaged during this cleaning process, they will be replaced with a new set of drapes (of the customer's choice) of equal value.

Presently, the majority of ready-made curtains are sold competitively in three types of stores: chains or discount stores, department stores, and furniture stores. The curtains in all these stores are priced competitively. One brand may be found in two or more stores. Some of the larger department stores have their own private-brand labels, which accounts for the bigger sales percentages shown in Exhibit 5.

Chain stores and department stores have relatively the same sort of display racks with size being the only difference. Curtains are already arranged on curtain rods over windows. All styles and colors are displayed, one right after another in the form of a room. At the base of each display "window" are separate packages of the corresponding curtain style for windows of various shapes.

The salespeople in charge of competitors' curtain departments are adequately trained to answer any pertinent questions asked by the curtain customer. The salespeople are trained by the companies who make the curtains to insure minimum breakdown of communication and trust between the manufacturer and the cus-

Exhibit 5   *Percentage increases of 1973 over 1966 sales of curtains*

Chain discount stores		*Average increase*
Yankee	10%	
Gibson's	8	
K Mart	7	
	25%	8%
Department Stores		
Grants	4%	
Federals	8	
Wards	12	
Hudsons	30	
	52%	13%
Furniture stores		
Art Van	4%	
Crown Furniture	3	
Gruenwalds	2	
Pruss	2	
	11%	3%

tomer. They are courteous and give hints to the customers on choices of styles and colors for the different rooms of a house.

Furniture stores also sell ready-made curtains, mainly for the dining room and bedroom. They offer discount prices, and the customer can match furniture with the drapery choice because the newly purchased furniture is right there. Many times, however, these stores do not carry quality items because curtains are a secondary item for them. They do not want to risk getting stuck with high-quality inventory when customer preference shifts to a different style or line.

Currently, there are no other specialty stores in Arlington or the surrounding area that also deal in ready-made curtains. Thus, no facts or figures are available to Mr. Gar to compare his estimates. All ready-made curtains would be purchased through a wholesale distributor.

Mr. Gar was asked by his sales force "who will be the target market?" He answered by saying that with the addition of ready-made curtains to the product line would come a willingness on the part of the construction home developers to let Kenley handle the complete job of installing the entire house with the necessary curtains and drapes. Presently, Kenley installs only the living room and door wall drapes for the majority of the model homes. With the addition of ready-made curtains, Kenley could also install the bedroom, dining room, kitchen, and utility rooms.

The addition of ready-made curtains might appeal to a steady customer or friend who wishes to deal at the store for something inexpensive. It would create goodwill among all income groups in the area.

Since Kenley Drapery Center is now known only for its quality by its customers, the people could now obtain a complete line of curtains at one store. Mr. Gar noted that this is an added convenience.

Advertising at Kenley is presently handled by an advertising agency. The agency works primarily on promotion of the high-quality draperies. As a result, customers regard Kenley as a specialty store and Gar does not want to lose this image. The ready-made curtains are not expected to carry the entire product line, but merely to be an added convenience for steady customers and to increase sales in the home construction market.

The store will have to sell ready-made curtains at a higher price than most of the competition because of added expenses. If a bedroom set of a ready-made product costs $16.99 in a department store, Kenley's price will be $18.59.

Question

Should Mr. Gar add ready-made curtains?

STILLWELL DISTILLERS

Paul Jonis is the head of the marketing department of Stillwell Distillers, a medium-sized distiller company. Recently, Mr. Jonis read an article in the *Wall Street Journal* concerning American drinking habits. The article pointed out that an increasing number of women and young adults drink regularly and that there is also a strong sense of "status" and "prestige" associated with certain brands. The demand for "light" liquor was growing rapidly. "Light" liquor is low in "proof" or alcoholic content and pale in color. It is also quite bland in taste and mixes readily with other beverages whose tastes the drinker prefers.

Mr. Jonis gave considerable weight to some statistics that were presented in the article. A chart reflected that in 1954, made-in-America whisky blends accounted for 42.6 percent of United States liquor sales and bourbon, 27.7 percent. More recently, those products had shrunk to 20.9 percent and 23.9 percent of the market respectively. Bourbon and blended whisky had long been the backbone of the distilling industry. Now they were losers. The gainers were vodka—a quintessential "light" liquor, because it is colorless and tasteless—scotch and Canadian whisky, both which are lighter in color than bourbon or United States blended whisky. Vodka had climbed to 11.2 percent of the market in 1969 from 1.8 percent in 1954. Scotch was up to 12.6 percent from 6.5 percent and Canadian whisky to 9 percent from 4.9 percent, during the same period. The social desirability of drinking had placed pressure on those people who do not like to drink. What they

Submitted by Paul Dunigan

wanted was something light that they could drink all night without tasting and without getting too drunk.

Mr. Jonis, after reading the article, was convinced that Stillwell should pursue development of a "light" liquor to compete against low-priced vodkas and imported Canadian whisky. Presently, the company produces two major brands of bourbon and one major brand of whisky. Although these products were successful and showed continuous sales growth, Mr. Jonis saw a need for a new product to catch up with some deep-seated changes in American drinking habits.

Mr. Jonis presented his new observations at the next staff meeting and persuaded the group to assign a special five-person committee to do further research. This research was to include the development of a whisky that satisfied the requirement discussed by the executive staff. The staff expected the product to have a mild whisky taste, to be unique, and to appeal to the young and well-educated.

Stillwell's marketing research department took some consumer attitude tests and found that people were attracted to a product that was clear in color and slightly whisky-tasting. This was determined by polls of individuals by mail and in person. Product research discovered that Sillwell could make something like that from what was already available for sale, and developed a liquor with these characteristics.

At the next executive staff meeting, the committee reported its findings. The committee stated that there was a definite market for the type of product that Sillwell researchers had developed. They recommended that the company move as fast as possible to establish a competitive advantage. Because of the remarkably high number of favorable responses, it was felt that further product research would not be necessary. Full-scale introduction should come next. It was felt by the staff that because liquor prices are fixed by law in most states, there was no need to do research on what people thought about value or price of the product.

The staff decided to name the product "Party Exchange." To Mr. Jonis, this name suggested fun and happiness. The traditional company bottle would be used. The company uses the same type of bottle for all of its major products. One of the directors thought that using the old bottle would help cut costs and create a favorable association between Party Exchange and the company's other liquors.

Stillwell executives knew that Party Exchange was the only light and clear whisky-tasting product on the market. Therefore, it was unique. Advertising was limited to the *Wall Street Journal, Business Week, Look,* and *Ebony.* Mr. Jonis knew that the average consumer had trouble distinguishing between types of liquor, much less brands. Consequently, to do lavish advertising would be foolish.

The product was introduced immediately on a full scale. Stillwell executives expected to sell about 75,000 cases the first year and 125,000 the second year.

After six months, the president of Stillwell, James Harris, called Mr. Jonis in to discuss what was happening to Party Exchange. Sales for six months were only 15,000 cases. Mr. Harris pointed out that the buyers of Party Exchange were the same customers who had been buying Stillwell's bourbon and blended whiskies. The prediction that Party Exchange would attract the young and well-educated was not being fulfilled. Mr. Harris had also heard that some whisky drinkers did not like Party Exchange because it looked like vodka and some vodka drinkers disliked it because it tasted like whisky. Mr. Harris did not want the company's reputation damaged. Marketing research revealed that young people have not been buying Party Exchange because the packaging does not appeal to them. In addition, many young people were unaware of the product. Only two out of ten were aware of the product. Fewer than that had tried it.

Sales have increased slowly, but have stayed relatively low in the northeastern part of the country. The biggest growth has been in the west.

Sales (in cases)

1st month	1000
2nd month	1500
3rd month	4000
4th month	2500
5th month	2500
6th month	3500
TOTAL	15,000

Current buyers have been heavily concentrated among those over forty years old, 75 percent being professional people.

It costs about $.30 per 4/5 quart to manufacture Party Exchange. If the product were dropped, the loss would be $3,000,000. There is still no similar product.

Question

> Should the product be continued? Justify your answer. Establish a procedure for determining when products should be dropped.

COMPONENT MANUFACTURING. INC,

The electric motor division of Component Manufacturing, Inc. had been manufacturing and selling a submersible motor that was very unreliable. It had a failure rate of about 9 percent. Component Manufacturing's competition operated with even more of a handicap: their failure rate was 13 percent. As a result of the failure rate, Component Manufacturing's submersible motor sales were not increasing as expected and service costs made a profitable operation almost impossible. The general sales manager for the electric motor division, Mr. John Abbott, wondered whether the submersible motors line should be dropped from the product mix.

Component Manufacturing, Inc., was a large manufacturer of a widely diversified assortment of products, most of which were sold to industrial markets. Except for a few small tools, the company had no experience with consumer products. Component Manufacturing had diversified both by acquiring existing companies and by expanding its own product lines. Sales last year for the total corporation were 650 million dollars. In addition to electrical components, the company made and marketed such products as industrial process control computers, elevators, steel fabricated products, and scales. With its home office in Pittsburgh, Pennsylvania, the company operated manufacturing facilities in four states and two countries.

It was the environmental movement that stimulated the demand for submersible motors and thus prompted Component Manufacturing to enter the market. Such motors were needed to pump

Submitted by Kenneth H. Dickey and Reginald A. Graham, Ph.D., Associate Professor of Business Administration, Fort Lewis College sewage and waste materials for proper disposal even though these motors had an abnormally high failure rate. Society would no longer allow the dumping of raw sewage into rivers and streams during mechanical failures.

The total market for the submersible motors was about $400,000 a year. Mr. Abbott felt that due to the unreliability and resulting low profitability of the product, the company should make a decision to either drop the product from the line or redesign it for greater reliability and manufacturing cost reductions. Thus, the decision was made to redesign the product with the objective of giving the product a competitive edge.

With this decision, the marketing department undertook a study to learn exactly what should be done to improve the product. Field trips to various municipalities, sewage pumping stations, and other pumping operations that use the product were taken. The main emphasis of the trips was talking with operating superintendents and studying applications of the product in an attempt to determine what the user would like in product performance.

The in-depth interviews of the marketing study indicated that both the users and the pump companies who manufactured the completed product had specific suggestions that would make the product more useful for them. The marketing department concluded that the product should be designed to the customer's specifications. Three of the features that they most wanted incorporated into the finished product were:

1. The motor should be explosion-proof. It should carry an Underwriters Laboratory label of the Class 1, Group D classification for operation in hazardous gases atmospheres. This feature recognizes the fact that a pitful of sewage could have anything from gasoline vapors to methane gas in it, both highly volatile. Therefore, if the motor was above the waterline, as opposed to being submerged (the normal operating condition), it would still be explosion-proof.
2. It was felt that the pump should have built-in safety features that would automatically shut the motor down in the event of overload, overheating, or seepage of water into the electrical chamber.
3. In the case of a shutdown, it was important that the reason for the stoppage be known. Therefore, it was suggested that monitors be installed at the top of the pit to tell the user what had caused the malfunction. This would allow the superintendent of pumping operations to make decisions based on current operating conditions. The superintendent could decide

whether to pull the motor and effect repairs immediately, or, via an override switch, to continue pumping, were there a critical situation. What is important here is that the superintendent should have the data necessary to analyze the situation based on the monitor readings at the top of the pit. With this information, an intelligent decision could be made at that point in time.

The marketing department took the study information, along with other new features felt to be important, to the research and design engineers. The design engineers were asked to design a product that contained all the suggested improvements and features.

The research and design engineers did a superb job of redesigning the product. A modern design, revolutionary in appearance, was created. Moreover, the new design demanded only a change in the external housing and now utilized standard internal parts. This meant that production costs could be held constant or perhaps even decreased.

Mr. Abbott and others in the marketing division were so favorably impressed with the new product that they asked production to build by hand twenty prototype motors. Marketing then asked four major pump companies to install pumps on the end of the motors for testing.

The motor-pump units were then installed at six different locations around the United States. At the end of approximately fifteen months, the motor-pump units were pulled out of the various pits around the country and returned to the Component Manufacturing laboratories for analysis. The results, based on the specific data available, projected that the new product would have a failure rate of less than one-half of one percent. Furthermore, Component Manufacturing, Inc., felt that it had a product that was totally reliable and that it could be installed for about 60 to 65 percent of the cost of alternative pumping methods.

After considering the above data, Mr. Abbott decided that Component Manufacturing, Inc., should deviate from their normal marketing policies for placing new products on the market — that is, from stocking only two or three units of each model. In this instance, the company was competing in an industry where quick turnaround time on orders was important, where cost savings were often passed on to the customer, and where any price increase was met with strenuous resistance.

Component Manufacturing, Inc., had only one direct competitor in the production and sale of submersible heavy-duty motors.

The market for this particular product was divided so that Component Manufacturing, Inc., controlled only about one-third of the sales. Their rival was larger and very aggressive and had superior contacts with the six or seven major pump companies, who were the primary prospects for submersible motors of this type. Mr. Abbott feared that any offensive selling tactics on his company's part would result in retaliation by this competitor. He also felt that both firms faced stiff competition from the twenty to twenty-five firms who manufactured substitute products — nonsubmersible motors that were attached to pumps via drive shafts.

Questions

If you were Mr. Abbott, what would be your first step to place the product on the market?

What type of pricing policy should Component Manufacturing, Inc., pursue in placing the new product on the market?

Does this product require any special inventory consideration?

If you were Mr. Abbott, is there any further information you might want? If so, what and from whom?

chapter 7

Distribution Cases

ZARB MANUFACTURING COMPANY
Replacing a Manufacturer's Representative

Zarb Manufacturing Company is a maker of automotive transmissions, power axles, heavy-duty construction equipment, and lift trucks. The main offices and several plants are located in northern Ohio. The company's products are sold throughout the United States and to some foreign countries. Selling is done either directly with the main office or through a manufacturer's representative, depending on the part of the country.

For the past fourteen years (1962–1976), Zarb's products sold in the northwestern region have been purchased through Robert C. Smith, a manufacturer's representative from Portland, Oregon. This region includes Oregon, California, Washington, Idaho, British Columbia, and Alaska. Mr. Smith has been a good representative for the Zarb Company. The following events affect the relationship between Zarb Manufacturing Company and Robert C. Smith, Inc., plus Zarb and its Northwest region.

May 5, 1976 — Zarb Manufacturing Company is officially notified of Mr. Smith's death, which occurred May 3, 1976. Robert C. Smith, Inc., wishes to fulfill their obligation as a representative for Zarb.

May 9, 1976 — Zarb writes a letter to Mr. Collins, a salesman for Smith, Inc., informing him that Zarb has sent letters to all accounts serviced by Smith, Inc., instructing them to continue buying through Smith until a new management is set up.

May 11, 1976 — The Zarb Company receives a letter from Coastal Car and Foundry Company, a buyer of Zarb products through Robert C. Smith, Inc. The letter states that since Mr.

Submitted by Donald Hoadley, District Circulation Manager, Jackson *Citizen Patriot*, Jackson, Michigan

Smith has passed away, Coastal would rather do business with Zarb directly.

May 16, 1976 — Zarb receives a letter from Tob Line Equipment Company, Portland, Oregon, which says that they would like to sell Zarb products.

May 17, 1976 — Stone Radiator Company writes to Zarb wanting to know the situation with Smith, Inc., since Smith also represents their firm.

May 18, 1976 — Yaggy Equipment Corporation, manufacturers and distributors of construction equipment, informs Zarb that it would like to represent Zarb in the Northwest region.

The following are replies from accounts serviced by Robert C. Smith, Inc., as to the method of handling their future account activities by Zarb. The replies have been analyzed by Zarb.

Puget Iron Works, Seattle, Washington: Puget is not that influential in our plans. They will abide by any distribution arrangement we decide upon. We must be sure of ourselves in our set up.

Coastal Car and Foundry: Coastal wishes to expand its business with Zarb through direct sales. They feel no manufacturer's representative is necessary.

Cates Manufacturing Co. Ltd., Vancouver, British Columbia: Cates will accept anything Zarb agrees upon.

Canadian Truck and Trailer Company Ltd., Vancouver, British Columbia: Canadian is a small account and thinks Zarb should not put emphasis on them. They were satisfied with Mr. Smith, but are unfamiliar with the other personnel in Smith, Inc. Canadian will go along with any Zarb decision. Canadian suggested that Zarb put an inventory of finished goods on the coast for quicker delivery.

Kingston Motor Truck, Seattle, Washington: Kingston has been satisfied with Mr. Smith's treatment of them, although in the last two years he has left their account up to Ms. Delores Dutton, an employee of Smith, Inc., who has been very cooperative with Kingston. They feel, however, that Zarb and Kingston can do business direct, and this would benefit both. Kingston does not want to take any credit away from Ms. Dutton; she has done a good job for them.

F. R. T. Cannon, Inc., Portland, Oregon: Cannon has begun to manufacture its own axles, so will no longer deal with Zarb in that department, but they will continue to buy transmissions from Zarb. These accounts will have to be handled directly.

Booth Manufacturing Company, Inc., Portland, Oregon: The Booth account will have to be handled directly and more economically.

Farrell Mining Scoop, Inc., Portland, Oregon: Farrell would prefer that the account be handled by Smith, Inc., but will accept any agreement made by Zarb.

The preceding replies were received by a Zarb representative in visits to each company, May 16–19, 1976.

June 3, 1976 — Zarb receives a letter from AMFAC, Inc., Honolulu, Hawaii. The letter informs Zarb that AMFAC has recently bought products from Ms. Dutton and they were very satisfied with her assistance. They hope Zarb will continue to sell through Smith, Inc., and Ms. Dutton in the future.

June 3, 1976 — Zarb writes to Mrs. Smith, new president of the firm telling her that they will continue to sell through Smith, Inc., if Mr. Collins will handle their products exclusively. Mr. Collins along with Mr. Smith primarily handled the Zarb account in the past.

June 7, 1976 — Ms. Dutton wrote to Zarb stating that she would like to continue representing them, either through Robert C. Smith, Inc., or by setting up her own firm. She feels she is experienced in working for Zarb.

June 7, 1976 — Mr. Maris, an executive of Robert C. Smith, writes to Zarb concerning their letter of June 3, which says Zarb will drop Smith, Inc., if Mr. Collins is not given the responsibility of Zarb's sales. Mr. Maris points out that his company has many employees capable of carrying the Zarb account. He states that Ms. Dutton currently accounts for 27½ percent of their business with Zarb, while Mr. Collins has 12½ percent. The remaining 60 percent of the business can be handled by other people in the firm. He feels both companies will benefit from a continued relationship.

June 13, 1976 — Stone Radiator Company writes to Zarb asking that Ms. Dutton be allowed to handle the Zarb account. Stone is in favor of retaining Ms. Dutton, and they think that Zarb and Stone should have the same representative for their products.

June 20, 1976 — The Zarb Manufacturing Company officially terminates its manufacturer's representative agreement with the Robert C. Smith, Inc., firm.

June 22, 1976 — Zarb receives a letter from Ms. Dutton stating that she has resigned from Robert C. Smith, Inc. She would like to discuss representing Zarb Automotive Division products in Washington and British Columbia.

June 25, 1976 — Mr. Collins writes Zarb informing them that he has resigned from Robert C. Smith, Inc. He states that he would like to continue representing Zarb from his own firm, Rollin Associates, Inc. If he continues to represent the company he would like to have Hawaii added on to the territory he has covered for Smith.

July 8, 1976 — Mr. Collins writes to Zarb telling them of the other companies which he is representing in hope of gaining the Zarb account.

July 13, 1976 — Zarb receives another letter from AMFAC Inc., which states that they still hope that Zarb retains Ms. Dutton as a representative.

July 16, 1976 — Zarb receives another letter from Ms. Dutton, which says that she is working with some other companies and she hopes Zarb will give her their account. Her firm is called Dutton Engineering Sales Company.

Additional information concerning Zarb Manufacturing Company and the northwest region follows.

Estimated sales, Northwest territory for 1976 — all divisions

Shipments January through April	$ 2,000,000
On order May through December	4,000,000
	$ 6,000,000
Additional estimated shipments in six available months	$ 400,000
	$ 6,400,000
Target	$ 7,000,000
Smith's December 1976 forecast	$10,500,000

Smith's shipments to May 1 and total 1976 orders as of May 1 (in $1000)

	January to April	May to December	1976
Smith less Collins	919	2844	3763
Collins	335	384	719
TOTAL	1254	3228	4482

Proposals for sales organization in Northwest territory (based on Collins' keeping present territory, northern California)

A. Oregon, Washington, and Vancouver, British Columbia, Salt Lake City, and Denver
   1. 31 customers
      a. Two outside salespeople
         One inside salesperson
         One service representative
         One stenographer
         Salaries and expenses $130,000
      b. Office equipment, telephone, TWX, duplicating   45,000
         First year estimated total expense $175,000

B. Portland and Seattle only (Salt Lake City and Denver)
   21 customers
   Two salespeople (1 Portland, 1 Seattle)
   One serviceperson (Portland)
   No office
   First year estimated
   total expenses $ 95,000

Northwest Territory Annual Sales Expense — Present System

	Commission	Sales target	
1971	$304,000	$ 6,400,000	
1972	545,000	7,200,000	$10,500,000
1973	416,000	8,335,000	estimate
1974	461,000	9,420,000	
1975	522,500	10,450,000	
1976	572,500	11,450,000	

1971 – 1976 total commission = $1,972,000
1979 only $1,025,000 commission based on $20,500,000 sales

Zarb could possibly sell direct to most of the concerns in the region, but many of the companies appreciate the personal contact with the salespeople. Even though the products being sold are industrial or component parts, each sale represents a substantial dollar amount and the personal effort can make a difference.

Zarb has used primarily manufacturing representatives in this region, but many of the customers would rather deal directly with Zarb. Zarb could lose a lot of business by declining to do business direct.

Zarb is a big name in this field and certainly draws many customers. Competition in the region has been combated in the past and Zarb will certainly keep this in consideration when determining its channel of distribution. Companies usually specify Zarb parts or other company equipment when they buy. Zarb will rely heavily on its established name in the region.

Zarb does use trade magazine advertising in an institutional manner, but it is not believed that such advertising takes the place of personal selling. Zarb will have to give the customers the kind of service they want. Zarb cannot rely solely on advertising.

Zarb does have its own sales force but they do mostly "missionary" work. They introduce companies to their products, leaving future ordering to be done through a manufacturing representative in the area. Some companies, if they are the only ones in the area buying Zarb parts, may order direct. Zarb has confidence in the manufacturing representative system and wants to use it wherever it is profitable.

Zarb has a very substantial truck fleet to meet its demand. It also has agreements with various trucking companies across the country concerning the delivery of Zarb products, if a company truck is not available. The actual production and delivery time is of utmost importance and Zarb realizes this. If the parts are not made and delivered in time, then a company is not going to have very many customers. There is intense competition in this field of industrial equipment.

Question

Who should represent Zarb in the Northwest territory? Justify.

MORT COMPANY
Balancing Service and Distribution Cost

J. W. Mort began producing the red paint on railroad cars in 1895. He expanded the company to a new area with the invention of the automobile. The automotive industry called upon Mort for undercoatings, sealants, and so on, to solve their wear problems. The company grew from one plant in Kankakee, Illinois, home office, to seven across the nation.

Mort protective products are seldom seen once they are applied, hence the name "the hidden protector." Mort is the manufacturer of technical coatings and sealants for the automotive, railroad, mobile home, truck and bus, appliance, and other metal fabricating industries. In addition, Mort produces and markets a complete line of proprietary consumer weatherstripping, condensation preventives, and sealants. These products prevent corrosion, deaden sound, retard flames, kill germs, and block wind, cold, and heat.

In 1954, Mort Company began feeling its way into the mobile home industry, with one distributor and one product, sealing tape. Eight years later, 1962, the Mobile Home Division was formed and a warehouse was located in Elkhart, Indiana — the mobile home capital of the world. Since that date, the mobile home industry has tripled in size, and so has Mort's breadth of line and product sophistication, a full line of sealants, adhesives, and coatings. And all mobile home products feature Mort's guaranteed and controlled delivery capability.

In Elkhart's mobile home industry, it has been the practice of suppliers to call regularly on the manufacturer to inventory stock

---

Submitted by Wendy Stock, Branch Bank Manager, Grand Rapids, Michigan

and write orders, thus alleviating one job for the purchasing agent. With the slow down of the economy in 1974, Mort questioned the necessity of calling on each customer two times per week. The Elkhart plant found they had to reduce costs. The salesperson called on forty plants, covering an area of approximately forty miles, and this involved 700 to 800 miles traveling time on his part. He had a company car and expense account and averaged $100 per week in expenses, plus gas. He had day-to-day routes which led to uniform delivery. The salesperson was being paid a salary of approximately $12,000, plus bonus and it was estimated that it cost the company $22,000 per year to keep him on the road. His sales did account for 60-65 percent of the total sales of the company. Small pick-up customers and customers of more than fifty miles away accounted for the rest. (Delivery was made only within forty miles of the warehouse; other orders were shipped by common carrier from the closest outlet.)

The Elkhart division has five employees at present. There are two drivers, one salesperson, one regional sales manager, and one office manager. The regional sales manager is responsible for Ohio, Kentucky, Indiana, Michigan, Minnesota, and Wisconsin. He calls on the one or two accounts in each state every month or every other month. His call frequency has been determined by the distance of the customer from Elkhart.

It is believed that most accounts would go along with a change to phone-in orders. Mort management realizes, however, that some purchasing agents through friendship or laziness would probably change suppliers. An estimated twenty accounts would be lost, out of 200 now being dealt with in the Elkhart area. Some of the major accounts might be among these, however. The salesperson was actually a glorified order-taker in this business and this function could easily be handled by the office manager by phone.

Attempts have been made to have the salesperson consolidate his small orders to cut costs. He must do $100 worth of business to make each call profitable. Thus, if the customers would buy $200 to $300 worth of merchandise at a time, it would pay both to have the salesperson and also to deliver the products. Since the salesman has been unable to obtain large orders, however, the company is attempting to cut back costs and still provide good service. It is felt that the companies supplied should be able to take their own inventory as others do in most industries.

Question

> Devise a plan to lower distribution cost for Mort Company, while still maintaining the same approximate level of service. Justify your plan.

UNITED GROCERS
Warehousing Location

In the summer of 1971, United Grocers, Inc., had signed a contract with McCann Company. This contract stated that United would stock and manage all of the food stores that would be opened adjacent to the Big M discount department stores. From 1971 until 1975, Big M and United opened 150 stores under the new agreement. The openings were becoming more frequent in the Michigan division and top management was considering the idea of moving and expanding its operations under one "roof."

History of United Grocers

United Grocers is a vast organization, operating approximately 400 supermarkets in the United States. One of the nation's "top 500" companies in sales volume, the growth of United is a success story in the tradition of the "American Dream." United had its beginning in 1941, when Henry and Ralph McGee opened a modest grocery store in midtown Detroit under the name of "Best Bet." From this initial outlet, "Best Bet" grew into a moderate-sized regional chain. By 1961, "Best Bet" was large enough to be incorporated and to be listed on the New York Stock Exchange. Five years later, the growth (caused by the absorption of other regional chains) had accelerated to the point where the "Best Bet" name was no longer appropriate for the company, and thus, in 1961, the company was reincorporated under the name of "United Grocers."

Submitted by Robert F. Kennedy, Market Analyst, Allied Supermarkets, Inc., Detroit, Michigan

Supermarket Divisions

Nationwide — United Discount Foods
United Grocers operates over two hundred supermarkets, principally under the name of Big M Food, in over thirty states.

Michigan — "Best Bet" Supermarkets
The parent division, now operates approximately eighty supermarkets. This division is now supplied by three warehouses which are located in the Detroit area.

Indiana — "Quality" Supermarkets
Nearly sixty supermarkets, including Indiana's largest chain of drugstores, are serviced by a large warehouse and distribution center in Indianapolis, Indiana.

Oklahoma, Texas, New Mexico — "Foodville" Supermarkets
A new warehouse and distribution center in Amarillo, Texas, supplies over thirty "Foodville" Supermarkets.

Wholesale Division

John Karras, Inc.
John Karras, Inc., a division of United, is one of America's largest and oldest companies supplying independent food retailers with their goods. Through John Karras, United actually "shares" its warehouse facilities with hundreds of independently-owned food stores. This business represents the spirit of helpfulness to smaller businesses, which is epitomized in the slogan "Come Shop With Us" blazoned on John Karras trucks and trailers, which have been seen for years on Michigan, Ohio, Illinois, and Indiana highways.

Michigan Division

As it was expected, United had enjoyed tremendous growth in the years following the contract signing with McCann. Some 150 stores had been added to the fold, and sales had more than doubled from $450 million to $950 million (see Exhibits 1 and 2).

With all of the new supermarkets opening in the Michigan Division combined with the present operations and all of the stores served by Karras, United is faced with over 300 large and small markets to supply. Some of these stores are in Indiana, Illinois, and Ohio, but they are near the Michigan state border. The warehouse facilities include a grocery and meat complex located in

Exhibit 1   *United Grocers annual sales*

Year	Sales
1975	$950,000,000
1974	$820,000,000
1973	$755,000,000
1972	$600,000,000
1971	$500,000,000
1970	$440,000,000
1969	$430,000,000
1968	$400,000,000
1967	$390,000,000
1966	$380,000,000
1965	$370,000,000
1964	$365,000,000

Exhibit 2   *Number of stores supplied*

Year	Units
1975	390
1974	380
1973	350
1972	315
1971	260
1970	245*
1969	240
1968	220
1967	210
1966	205
1965	175
1964	150

the same area as the headquarters, a non-food warehouse two miles southeast of the headquarters, and a produce warehouse eight miles southeast of the headquarters near the Detroit River and near all major produce distribution centers serving all of the food stores in Detroit. All of the ordering for the stores is processed through the computer system, located in the headquarter offices (see Exhibit 3).

The warehouses that United now runs are not adequate for the expanding Michigan division. Besides being scattered, they are run down and will need to be repaired and generally cleaned up. Management has suggested a minimum price of at least $4 million to refurbish the existing structures. It has been determined that a new location could be established that would be able to

*Including "Big M" units.

house the entire distribution and maintenance center. A center could be built in the Detroit suburb of Warren. This suburb is a mixture of industrial and residential sections. There is a population of over 100,000 people which could be easily tapped for labor. Besides centralizing the operations of the Michigan Division, such a complex would allow room to engage in other enterprises that United cannot now handle. As it stands now, it is imperative that management make a decision to build or rebuild.

If built, a new facility would be capable of housing the grocery, non-food, meat, produce, and dairy warehouses. There should be plenty of room to engage in the manufacturing of products that the company now purchases through distributors. These would include: milk and milk by-products, breads, salads, and snacks. A new complex would require about 1,000,000 square feet in order to house these various warehouse and manufacturing operations. An additional 300,000 square feet of property to house additional offices would also be needed. This would represent an area about double the size of the present facilities.

Exhibit 3   United Grocer facilities: metropolitan Detroit

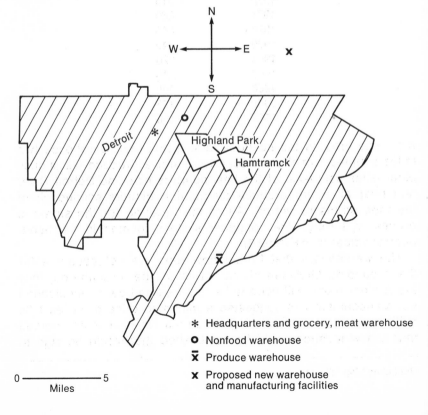

* Headquarters and grocery, meat warehouse

O Nonfood warehouse

X̄ Produce warehouse

X Proposed new warehouse and manufacturing facilities

0 ———————— 5
        Miles

The new complex would be located very near the geographic center of Warren, Michigan, thirteen miles northeast of the present headquarters site. The location would be next to an existing railroad track for easy transportation movement. It is also in the population center of the city for easy access to a large working force.

The Warren complex would be leased from the city of Warren. The total price of the lease contract would come to approximately $11,000,000 per year. This price would be offset by the sales of manufactured products by the complex, and by the savings that could be attained through a centralized company.

The 300 stores in the Michigan Division could be served more rapidly by a centralized warehouse complex. It could also serve more of the stores in the near outlying areas that are now served by the Indiana distribution centers or by independent warehouses and distribution centers.

The competition in the Michigan Division consists of seventeen chains in the Detroit and Michigan areas and numerous small independents. The other major chains in Detroit are Kroger, A & P, National and Food Fair supermarkets, all doing around $15 million of food retailing business in the Detroit area alone per week.

The main promotional campaigns of the competition are discount pricing and heavy advertising in newspapers. The discount pricing has been attained by dropping the cost of trading stamps and ordering goods in larger quantities. It is *assumed* United could save money by centralizing its operations, thereby reducing prices.

It is believed that the old warehouses could be easily disposed of, since they are located in the industrial and very valuable section of Detroit. In fact, the location (Detroit) is excellent, but consolidating the warehouses in one area is impossible because of the inavailability of land in one location. The warehouses could also be leased to smaller companies who would occupy small sections of present structures.

Questions

> Establish a procedure for determining optimum warehouse location. Justify your procedure.
>
> What are the major considerations in warehouse location?
>
> What should United do?

THE GRIND FINE COMPANY
Selecting Channels of Distribution

Mr. Stanley C. Sower, the newly elected President of Grind Fine Company, was considering methods by which the Grind Fine Company could improve its share of the market for finishing equipment. Mr. Sower was also concerned with the declining profit margin that the company had experienced in recent years.

Founded in 1940, the Grind Fine Company began operations as a supplier of natural stones for use in tumbling barrels. The tumbling barrels were used to deburr, polish, clean, burnish, and in other ways prepare metal parts for a finishing operation, such as painting or plating. Granite and limestone was purchased in carload lots and sorted into sizes by a screening operation.

The company developed an excellent reputation for quality stones and was moderately successful. During the second world war, a number of customers of stones requested that the Grind Fine Company supply tumbling barrels. An agreement with a small metal working company was made to produce the barrels.

After the war, the metal working company expressed a desire to sell the tumbling barrel manufacturing facilities to Grind Fine Company. An agreement was worked out and Grind Fine Company started to manufacture their own tumbling barrels in 1949.

Growth of the company continued to be above average for the next years. New inventions in vibratory deburring equipment allowed the Grind Fine Company to hold a fair share of the market. In the early 1960s, business was declining because of high costs and severe competition.

Submitted by Laurie Bergerson, Vice President-Treasurer, Roto-Finish Company, Kalamazoo, Michigan

Fortunately for Grind Fine Company, a new round machine was patented by the son of the founder in 1965. The new machine, called the "Grindatron," proved very successful and virtually eliminated tumbling barrels and vibratory equipment.

Sales volume and profits were satisfactory until 1973, when operating profit fell to 3.4 percent. Operating losses were experienced in 1974 and 1975.

Exhibit 4   *Sales and operating profit for last five years*

	1971	1972	1973	1974	1975
Sales	$2,317,500	$2,684,000	$3,106,700	$3,627,000	$1,906,900
Operating profit (loss)	228,400	254,200	104,600	(62,000)	(258,000)
Percent of sales	9.85	9.47	3.37	(1.7)	(13.52)

The entire picture of the deburring business had changed in the preceding ten to fifteen years. The "Grindatron" had changed the equipment line and the natural granite and limestone stones had been replaced by preformed ceramic and plastic media. Whereas natural stones were previously sorted to desired sizes, the new preformed media were made to a specific size and shape.

"Preforms" were made by mixing a specific amount of an abrasive with either ceramic clay or plastic resin. Because the preformed media were synthetic, it was possible to manufacture the media in a number of various shapes or forms, such as triangles, spheres, cones, and cylinders. It was also possible to make the media so that it deburred fast or slow, depending on the type of results desired. By 1971, the Grind Fine Company had discontinued the use of natural stones and manufactured only preformed media. The few orders received for natural stones were handled under an agreement with a supplier in Wisconsin.

In 1952, dry compounds were introduced for use in the tumbling barrels and vibratory equipment in order to keep the stones clean. The dry compounds were also used in the "Grindatron," but because of the continuous action, a liquid compound was found to be better suited. Several liquid compounds were introduced in 1972 and were immediately successful.

Exhibit 5 presents the breakdown of Grind Fine Company sales for the past five years.

The loss in 1974 was attributed to failure to adjust prices on the equipment line for the past three years. Continued material and labor cost increases were not covered by increased productivity or price increases. It was assumed that approximately

Exhibit 5   *Grind Fine Company sales by product line*

	1971	1972	1973	1974	1975
Natural stones	$ 53,400	$ 28,900	$ 92,400	$ 98,000	$ 60,700
Plastic media		115,900	174,700	223,900	137,000
Ceramic media	299,100	268,800	357,400	319,900	230,400
Dry compound	328,400	280,100	233,300	223,400	191,900
Liquid compound		140,000	197,800	232,700	209,700
Grindatron	1,328,900	1,481,000	1,545,200	1,899,400	768,500
Other equipment	67,300	171,900	230,000	328,300	79,800
Spare parts	240,400	197,400	275,900	301,800	228,800
	$2,317,500	$2,684,000	$3,106,700	$3,627,100	$1,906,900

a yearly loss of 2 percent had resulted from failure to adjust prices. The average price of a "Grindatron" was $11,000, with costs averaging 30 percent for material and 15 percent for direct labor and manufacturing overhead. Because of reduced volume in 1974, the average cost of direct labor and manufacturing overhead increased to 26 percent of sales. In mid-1975, the equipment prices were adjusted to reflect current cost levels.

The material costs for media and compounds were 40 percent of sales, with labor and overhead averaging 10 percent. Gross profit before distributor discount, selling expense, and indirect manufacturing overhead and administrative expense was 50 percent for media and compounds and 55 percent for equipment. Advertising expenditures were restricted to equipment and averaged 2½ percent of equipment sales.

Prior to being elected President, Mr. Sower was the Vice-President of Sales for the Grind Fine Company. He had held this position for the last eleven years. For the six years prior to being named the Vice-President of Sales, Mr. Sower had been a salesperson for the company.

The Grind Fine Company marketed its products through regional distributors who were paid a commission of their sales. Commissions, or discounts, ranged from 10 percent on equipment to 23½ percent on media and compounds. The equipment commission was increased to 15 percent if the distributor purchased a "Grindatron" for use as a demonstrator to show potential customers. Approximately half of the distributors owned demonstrators and qualified for a 15 percent discount. The distributors were supposed to handle all customer contact, but the degree of service offered by individual distributors varied from practically zero to complete coverage.

In 1963, when Mr. Sower became Vice-President of Sales, over 50 percent of the total sales volume of Grind Fine Company was routed through one distributor. This distributor provided very little service to customers, so Grind Fine was forced to hire a full-time serviceperson to install equipment and make repairs. No change in distributor discounts was made as a result of this work undertaken by Grind Fine Company.

Mr. Sower started in 1965 to obtain additional distributors in order to reduce the percentage of business generated by the one distributor. He also started to look for qualified people to become sales engineers for the Grind Fine Company. It was his intention to reduce the dependency of the Grind Fine Company on the activities of one distributor, if at all possible.

By the beginning of 1975, the Grind Fine Company had four full-time sales engineers who worked with distributors rather than on a direct basis. Nearly all sales credited to a sales engineer were also credited to the distributor in that area. Distributors operating in the South and west of the Mississippi did not receive any aid from sales engineers. One sales engineer operated out of Chicago and covered Illinois and Wisconsin. One sales engineer covered Michigan and Northern Indiana. Ohio, Southern Indiana, and part of Kentucky were the responsibility of a third sales engineer and the New England states and New York City were covered by another sales engineer. All these areas were also covered by distributors.

The fixed cost of a sales engineer averaged $17,500 and covered such items as base salary, car allowance, and road expenses. Commissions of 2 percent were paid on all sales credited to sales engineers. The annual commisions varied from year to year because of volume changes, but averaged about $8,000 per sales engineer.

Approximately two-thirds of all sales were credited to sales engineers for commission purposes. Distributor discount was paid on nearly all sales. The direct expense of distributor and sales engineers is present in Exhibit 6.

As Mr. Sower reviewed the 1975 profit and loss statement, he wondered if the company would do better without distributors in the areas covered by sales engineers. Certainly there was a duplication of effort which was costing Grind Fine Company an extra

Exhibit 6   *Distributor discounts and expense of sales engineers*

Year	Sales	Distributor discount	Percent of sales	Sales engineer commission
1971	$2,317,500	$255,700	11.0	$32,200
1972	2,684,000	346,700	12.9	35,600
1973	3,106,700	395,800	12.7	41,300
1974	3,627,100	491,500	13.6	50,100
1975	1,906,900	289,400	15.2	27,700

amount. Mr. Sower also remembered that before he added the sales engineers the volume of sales had dropped and the Grind Fine Company was dependent on one distributor for over 50 percent of the sales volume. In 1974, that same distributor had less than 25 percent of the total sales volume.

The distributor covering New York City and the New England states had taken on a competitive line of supplies in April, 1974. This action was in violation of the distributor agreement signed with Grind Fine Company. Mr. Sower would have to take action and most likely dismiss the distributor, since he had no intention of eliminating the competitive line. Another qualified distributor would be dfficult to find and would take months to train once acquired.

Six months prior, the eastern area Sales Manager for a competitor had approached Mr. Sower for a position. Mr. Sower interviewed the woman and was favorably impressed. The economic picture at that time did not permit a job offer, but Mr. Sower left an opening for future possibilities.

This salesperson was capable of taking over the eastern area and directly supervising the current sales engineer. If Mr. Sower hired the competitor's sales manager, it would help relieve Mr. Sower's current load, since he was still responsible for sales even though he was now President. It might even be possible to operate in the New England/New York City area without a distributor. If this system was successful in this one area, it could be expanded to other areas later.

The distributor discount earned by the distributor in the New York City and New England states area was as follows:

Year	Sales	Distributor discount	Percent of sales
1973	$539,881	$91,127	16.9
1974	581,312	99,400	17.1
1975	209,278	38,300	13.6

As he studied the various reports, it occurred to Mr. Sower that if no distributor discount had been paid in 1974 and 1975, the Grind Fine Company would have had a profit in those years. He believed that the sales volume in the areas covered by sales engineers would not decline more than 10 to 25 percent if he dropped the distributors and sold direct. He also believed if he doubled the number of sales engineers for the current areas, that the loss of sales would be very minor, less than 10 percent. It was the areas not covered by sales engineers that would experience a large decline in sales if he dropped the distributors. Approximately one-quarter to one-third of the total sales volume was generated by those distributors.

A Board of Directors meeting was scheduled for the end of the month and Mr. Sower wanted to present a definite proposal at that time.

Questions

Should Grind Fine distribute its products through its own sales force, through distributors, or by some other arrangement?

What should Grind Fine do about the distributor's carrying a competing product?

How will a change in distribution affect the Grind Fine organization?

chapter

8

Communications in Marketing Cases

C & W POOL CONSTRUCTION COMPANY
Establishing Middleman's Promotional Strategy

Mr. Charles Williams is owner and operator of C & W Pool Construction Company, located in Oshkosh, Wisconsin. He has been associated with the pool industry for the past seven years and is well-versed in the area of construction and servicing of pools. He is a member of the National Swimming Pool Institute.

Today, swimming pools are a big business, potential buyers being in the $9,000 a year (and up) income group. In the 1950s, backyard pools were almost nonexistent. By 1958, the total of all types of swimming pools in the United States was only 184,000. This year there are nearly one million home pools in the ground and many more than that above ground.

The factory prebuilt vinyl-liner pool, invented in 1954, has been a key factor in this rapid expansion. This has brought swimming to a family's backyard, for about the cost of a moderately-priced car.

Mr. Williams represents Wolf Pools Corporation of Sark, Pennsylvania, a very reputable pool manufacturer for twelve years. In 1975, Charles Williams had five employees installing pools for him and was making plans to expand in 1976. He sold twenty-six pools in 1975 on the basis of referrals from previous customers with very little promotional effort. Mr. Williams would like to sell forty-five pools in 1976 and recognizes the need for a sound plan of promotion to accomplish this goal. Mr. Williams operates with very little overhead. When he sells a pool, he picks it up from the Wolf Distributor in Chicago and delivers it directly to the job site. He likes to finish the job in two weeks from the date of purchase.

Mr. Williams is the sole salesperson for C & W and often finds himself without any customer leads.

Wolf Pools Corporation manufactures a complete line of rectangular and free-form vinyl liner pools. These pools range in size from twelve feet by twenty-four feet to twenty-four feet by forty-eight feet, or larger on special order. There are two types of walls available by Wolf, metal or wooden. The pool may be installed above ground or in the ground. The walls of the pool are supported by Perm-X-Braces, a patented brace used in the pool industry only by Wolf Pool Corporation, one Perm-X-Brace every four feet on the rectangular pool. The braces are anchored back by concrete; this makes it possible to drain the pool without any worries of wall cave-ins. The vinyl liner is similar to other liner pools, constructed of twenty-gauge vinyl. The liner is guaranteed for ten years on a declining basis for replacement cost. Overall, the Wolf Pool is a well-constructed pool. It is sold in a complete kit, to be installed by a dealer or the consumer.

The pools from Charles Williams' competitors in the Oshkosh area can be categorized into three main classes of materials: (1) gunite or concrete, (2) vinyl liner with fiberglass walls, and (3) vinyl liner with steel walls. The advantages and disadvantages of the various forms of pools can be seen in Exhibit 1.

The gunite or concrete dealers consist of Oshkosh Swim Pool Company and Johnson Pool Company. Vinyl liner with fiberglass walls are sold by Vlietstra Brothers Swim Pool Company and Coak Construction and Home Improvement Enterprises. Vinyl liner with steel walls are sold through Eldorado Pools of Oshkosh, Sun 'n' Swim Center, and C & W Pool Construction.

The geographic area Mr. Williams is interested in is the city of Oshkosh and surrounding suburban areas. Mr. Williams has gone as far as seventy miles to install a pool for special reasons, but he doesn't wish to do this very often. He feels that, if he must travel more than twenty miles to a job, it will be very difficult to furnish adequate service to the customer in the future.

The income classes C & W tries to reach are middle-income to upper-income classes. The reasoning behind this is that middle-income customers are usually paying for a home, perhaps a car, all on monthly installments. These people have established a good credit rating and run into very little problem obtaining funds from their banks or local finance companies for the purchase of a pool. Also, the lending institution actually takes very little risk because a swimming pool will raise the value of the customer's property, thus increasing the collateral. The upper-income classes generally have money saved and need not worry about financing their pool. This saves time on Mr. Williams' part, because he normally helps

Exhibit 1   Product comparison

Pool types	Structural strength	Shape	Interior finish	Initial cost	Normal annual maintenance cost	Problems
Form-poured concrete	Good with adequate steel reinforcements	Rectangular	Fair	$4,500 6,000	$250 – $300	Cracking, leaking
Pneumatically applied concrete (gunite)	Very good with adequate steel reinforcement	All shapes	Fair	5,000 6,500	$250 – $350	Cracking, leaking
Dry-pack concrete	Fair with adequate steel reinforcement	All shapes	Fair	3,500 6,000	$250 – $300	Cracking, leaking, sloping walls
Concrete block	Fair	Rectangular	Poor	2,500 4,500	$100 – $150	Cracking, leaking, early deterioration
Brick	Fair	Varied	Poor	4,000 5,500	$100 – $150	Cracking, leaking
Steel	Excellent	All shapes	Excellent	5,000 6,500	$200 – $225	Might deflect
Aluminum	Excellent	All shapes	Excellent	5,500 6,500	$150	Might deflect, pitting
Fiberglass walls, concrete floor	Excellent	All shapes	Excellent	4,500 6,500	$70	None
Vinyl-lined steel walls	Excellent	Various	Excellent	3,000 5,500	$70	None
Vinyl-lined aluminum	Good	Rectangular	Excellent	2,500 4,000	$70	May "pit" in time, causing liner damage
Vinyl-lined wood walls	Excellent	Rectangular	Excellent	2,500 4,000	$70	Wolmenization may not be applied correctly (Cypress does not require this)

133

with finance arrangements and this frees him for other aspects of the business.

C & W Construction would like to stress *quality* in its advertising because of the patented Perm-X-Braces used in the building of Wolf Pools. With this single feature they can claim to be "the strongest name in pools." The "X" shape is used in construction where strength is required. Mr. Williams also does a little advertising on service, and this generally concerns pool supplies — such as chemicals, winterizing pools in the fall, and opening them in the spring. Williams stays away from publishing prices, because he appraises every job individually, each being unique. This practice could result in price differences. Mr. Williams does not know how much he wants to spend on promotion.

Wolf Pool Corporation supplies its dealers with advertising mats for newspapers, pamphlets, and handouts to tell the public about Wolf Pools. They send out up-to-date ideas concerning media usage and when to advertise. There is no reimbursement program set up by Wolf Pool Corporation for local advertising. They justify this by sending dealers free advertising supplies.

Wolf Pool Corporation carries out a nationwide promotional program in the spring and fall each year. The spring program consists of a price reduction to dealers so they may pass the savings on to the public. This gets the seasonal pool business in this part of the country into full swing. In the fall they might give a free heater or pool cover to each purchaser, to lengthen the purchasing season of the pool business. The spring promotion runs in the month of April and the fall promotion in September each year. Wolf Pool Corporation does a small amount of magazine advertising during the summer months, but these advertisements only tell the name—Wolf Pools—with little information on the product.

Questions

> Establish a promotional strategy for C & W Pools. Justify your strategy.
>
> Evaluate the Wolf promotional program.

SON PRINTING COMPANY
Promoting a Small Service Firm

The Son Printing Company of Salisbury, Maryland, is a family-owned commercial job printing shop which has been in operation for approximately fifty years. The bulk of its products are made up of cards, letter forms, envelopes, business forms, specification sheets, and advertising folders and posters. The market segments presently reached include industrial printing, retail printing, personal printing, and institutional printing. Due to the size and potential of the business, the market area is contained in a fifteen-mile radius, including Wicomico County. At present, the company has about 200 customers. It was felt the potential of the facilities and its employees was not being reached. It was not a matter of laziness, but the operation could be put to fuller use. Increasing the operation's clientele to 300 customers, through advertising and a salesperson, would put the firm at capacity.

The business contains four letter presses, and two offset presses, with additional photographic and cutting machinery. If the job requires certain steps or machines not contained in Son Printing, that work is subcontracted to the closest facility. Usually if subcontracting is known to be involved beforehand, the job will be refused. There are six full-time employees, and three part-time. The business operates five to six days a week, on a nine to five schedule. The peak periods are the months of December through March, or usually when the customers restock after inventory.

Through the years, the business has changed little. The owners, a husband and wife, began the business in 1923. Now most of the operation is handled by the son, a college graduate with a degree in printing management.

Submitted by Kenneth L. Otte, Press Relations, Texas Instruments, Inc., Dallas

The sales figures for the past few years show a general increase in total sales dollars, with a steady increase in expenses. It was suggested that the greatest benefits might be obtained through expense-cutting. Price rates have not changed to any great degree through the years.

Exhibit 3   *Sales and expense figures*

	Sales volume	Expenses	Profit
1968	$77,000	$76,500	$ 500
1969	79,000	78,000	1,000
1970	88,000	84,000	4,000
1971	79,000*	75,000*	4,000*

*Through August 1971 only

Expense breakdown for 1970

Wages	$45,000
Supplies	30,000
Maintenance	5,000
General expenses	3,700
Advertising and promotion ..	300

Industry and Competition

There are two companies in direct competition with Son Printing — College Press and Imperial Printing. They are also located in Salisbury, within two miles of Son. They service the same market area, with basically the same product line. Due to the size of these three printing companies and available promotional techniques, the market areas are fairly concentrated, and no surrounding printing companies outside Wicomico County need to be recognized as being in direct competition with Son Printing.

The competitors are also family-owned operations in existence for several years. Their activities in the area of advertising and promotion could be termed very conservative, as compared with other industries. The printing business is usually unaggressive in promotional efforts, perhaps because of their size in total sales dollars and the expense involved. Copying competitors' promotional practices is extremely easy, making it difficult to differentiate a firm's image. The only real advertising that is carried out at Son is direct-mail, at a cost of about $60 per year, and a subscription in the yellow pages of the phone book, at the standard cost of $200 per year. Both are mainly directed at the professional individuals, with some attention to personal service.

It has been shown by a survey that there are two basic reasons sales lag for small and localized printing companies: (1) too many printing companies offering the same products and services and (2) confusion in the minds of potential customers of what a printing company can offer. In the same survey it was shown that the average amount spent on printing per year is $600 for professional needs, and $100 for personal and civic needs.

Product Distribution

Since Son Printing only services a small area, the product distribution is not very extensive. Seventy-five percent of the total volume is sold to professional companies within the Salisbury area, and the remaining volume — 25 percent — is distributed between personal service and civic needs within the community. Order-taking is normally by phone, walk-in, or by letter; no sales personnel are utilized. Most of the business is repeat, and the customer usually knows exactly what he wants before ordering. Impulse buying is not a major factor in sales.

One of the young employees at the company made the following suggestions:

1. Increase the present advertising expenditure from less than ½ percent of total yearly sales ($300 in 1970) to 2 percent of total yearly sales ($1,500), in the hope of increasing profit by expanding the desire for and knowledge of Son Printing's product. It is also hoped that this would double the market coverage, from a fifteen-mile radius (200 customers) to a thirty-mile radius (with possibly 300 customers).
2. Introduce one salesperson to Son Printing, for the purpose of soliciting orders and supplying information and assistance to potential customers in their market area. Recently an individual had applied for a sales job with Son Printing, but the owners were hesitant about hiring a salesperson.
3. Introduce a specialty item to differentiate Son Printing from competitors (yearly annual report printing). A substantial amount of the advertising budget would be utilized along these lines, for the purpose of informing businessmen of this service. It is also suggested that the salesperson concentrate efforts in this area, making presentations to company executives of the ideas that could be initiated by Son Printing.

These suggestions were made by the employee, based upon his perception of the Son operation. Some of his perceptions are:

(1) In recent years there has been a change from companies doing their own printing to securing commercial job-printing companies to fulfill their needs. As far as personal printing, more and more individuals are having commercial printers supply them with their cards, letters, etc., for holiday, and everyday use. There is a definite increase in demand for commercial printing, justifying an increase in expenditures. (2) At the present time, Son is meeting all expenses that occur. The three so-called executives of the business are making $15,000 each per year. It is believed by management, however, that the additional advertising allowance and salesperson's wages would cut into their gross profit. (3) No increase in price of any item is intended. A price rate will have to be established for the yearly annual report printing. (4) The major growth market is the professional individual. (5) The advertising campaign will definitely improve the company image, especially if some institutional advertising can be utilized. Son can and should increase their activities in community affairs — such as sponsoring activities and contributing promotional materials.

Question

Evaluate the promotional suggestions made and develop one-year and five-year promotional programs for Son Printing.

ROWS CORPORATION
Reorganizing the Sales Force

Justification of Problem

The Portsmouth, New Hampshire, branch of Rows Corporation was faced with a problem that would have a powerful impact on the future success of the branch and management team during the coming years. This would be the first major change in marketing procedures in over ten years, and it was anticipated that this change—if implemented—would be in effect for years to come.

During the years 1975 and 1976, Rows Corporation was forced to develop new and more efficient marketing methods. The primary reason for this pressure was the increased sophistication both of its data-processing equipment and of customers' awareness of the field. This necessity for a shift in marketing strategy was evident to the branch manager and sales manager in the Portsmouth branch of Rows Corporation. Since the sales staff in the branch was relatively young and three new members had recently been added, it was decided that September, 1976, would be a good time to install a new marketing program.

Corporate Background

Rows Corporation, headquartered in Chicago, was founded in 1891, soon after the invention of the adding machine. From the sale of the first machine, Rows has grown to one of the world's largest corporations with 1975 sales of $893 million and income

Submitted by Michael Allers, Product Management, World Headquarters, Detroit

of $132 million before taxes. Rows is rated as being one of the fastest-growing companies in the nation today. Sales in the last ten years have risen from $401 million to $893 million in 1975. Net income per share has risen in the same period from $.79 per share to $3.83 per share in 1975. For the first three quarters of 1976, income was up 10 percent from the previous year, and this in a year that is generally agreed to be economically unfavorable.

A Thrace & Company report of August 9, 1976 reads, "We believe Rows to be in the best position among the mainframe computer makers to capitalize on the improved computer industry conditions we foresee for 1977 . . . In our opinion, Rows has developed the broadest EDP product line next to IBM, consisting of minicomputers selling for as little as $10,000 up to super-sized computers selling for millions of dollars."

Rows Corporation operates worldwide with branches in over 132 countries and a field staff of over 20,000 sales, service, and technical support personnel. The Business Machines Group, of which Portsmouth is a part, consists of sixteen district offices and 249 branch offices. These branches range in size from twenty-five people to over 1,000 people, depending on the metropolitan area being serviced and the products being supported. Portsmouth has twenty-five people with eight of these being sales people and the rest being either office personnel or field engineers.

Product Line

One of the primary reasons for considering a shift in marketing emphasis is the drastic change in new products. During the years up to 1975, the saleperson's primary concern was the sale and installation of electromechanical accounting equipment. Even though he or she had responsibility for the sale of adding machines and calculators, the greatest portion of the commission was made on the larger Series F and E equipment. This equipment was limited in that it could not do an adequate job where typing of alpha descriptions (name and address on payroll checks or voucher checks) was necessary, and many times could not provide the customer with all the information required. For example, a nineteen total (top of the F line) accounting machine was impractical when the state of Illinois instituted state withholding tax on payroll. Although the Series E equipment could multiply and divide, it was mechanically operated and greatly increased the amount of "downtime" a customer would have.

From the salesperson's standpoint, the F's and E's were easier to program and install because they were limited in capability and required less technical knowledge.

Exhibit 4 Product Mix

Product group	Series	Description	# of styles	Prices		Quantity — Dollars sold 1/75, 11/76	
Group I	J	Ten-key adding machine	16	$ 139 –	$ 299	65 –	$ 9,392
	P	Full-key adding machine	35	199 –	830	32 –	11,421
	10	Cash machines	7	239 –	595	7 –	1,959
	C	Calculators	25	379 –	1,795	74 –	33,335
Group II	F	Electromechanical accounting machines	62	2,150 –	8,690	14 –	55,550
	P–9	Desk-model posting machines	14	690 –	1,190	1 –	1,165
	P–7	Tellers machines	12	790 –	1,490	19 –	11,465
	E	Electronic accounting systems	50	5,990 –	24,900	5 –	46,088
	L	Accounting computers	41	6,995 –	27,050	13 –	136,634
Group V	N	Magnetic tape encoders	23	4,990 –	36,455	6 –	7,630
	S	MICR encoders	7	2,995 –	14,499	10 –	22,320
	A	Keypunch, sorters	8	3,140 –	6,380	2 –	9,130
Group VI	TC	Terminals	23	7,590 –	15,990	6 –	28,483
	B–9	Display terminals	33	8,580 –	11,000	0 –	000
	TU	On-line tellers	39	2,640 –	7,300	0 –	000
	RT	Remote tellers	9	7,490 –	19,490	0 –	000
Group VIII	TA	Data sets	13	590 –	6,200	5 –	2,110
	DC	Data communications Controller	14	19,200 –	100,920	0 –	000
Group III	B	Medium- and large-scale data processing systems	—	Always lease		5 –	369,543

Note: Exhibit 4 does not include the sales from several product groups, peripheral equipment, and software. It should be noted that the Series E and L systems, and the Group V, Group VI, and Group VIII systems are available with over 200 peripheral devices that greatly increase the number of styles and configurations available.

With the release of the Series L family of minicomputers, marketing problems arose that branch offices had not had to contend with before. Because the machine was "soft," the salespeople now had to be familiar with software (programming) and had to be especially conscious of the equipment's capabilities. The Series L is completely internally programmed and comes available with a complete array of subsystems, such as paper tape, punch card, line printers, and terminals.

Now the customer could ask and expect more results because she or he was not limited as much by the machine's capabilities as by personal imagination. This presented a very real problem to the salesperson, since the objective was to sell an efficient system, but at the same time free the salesperson from the programming, installation, and system design as quickly as possible.

During the years 1975 and 1976, all of the new products were revolutionary in design and in many cases required the setting up of new product groups. Groups V, VI, and VIII were brought into being during this period of time. By August of 1976, two facts became very clear:

1. The new products could be installed faster than the old, if they were sold on standard programs, and they would require less of the salesperson's time once the system was thoroughly understood.
2. It was humanly impossible for any one salesperson to understand all the products and have a working knowledge of the standard systems on each.

Sales
Personnel

The Portsmouth Branch had six salespeople in August of 1976. The staff was quite young, with the oldest person having been with the company 2½ years. Four of the staff had been hired during 1976. Because of the newness of the people involved and because they would have few territory preferences, it was decided to instigate a new marketing program during September of that year.

In the past, the salespeople were divided up into six equal geographic territories with each person having full product and customer responsibility within the territory. They were paid salaries and graduated commissions based on sales for a calendar twelve-month period.

It was estimated that a salesperson spent about 30 percent to 40 percent of the time in front of a customer selling new equipment. The balance of the time was spent designing systems, programming, installing new equipment, training operators, and doing the necessary paperwork to maintain the territory. With the release of the new products and with a limited amount of practical experience with them, it was assumed that the time spent selling new equipment would be reduced. This was, in essence, the problem facing the nationwide network of Rows branches.

Systems Design

Rows Corporation has always been of the philosophy that if a salesperson proposes an efficient system to the customer, the machine's sale is automatic.

With this in mind, the company had provided just about every tool a salesperson could want when presenting a system proposal to a prospective customer. System brochures, flowcharts, ready-made programs, system documentations, and sample forms were always ready—whether the salesman was calling on a hospital, credit union, auto dealer, bank, or governmental unit. The company was able to do this because each Series F and E machine had certain characteristics that lent itself to a specific application.

With the new equipment, however, it was becoming increasingly difficult to standardize programs and advertising because of the tremendous flexibility of the equipment. The salespeople also had trouble learning more than a few of the systems because of the comprehensiveness of the programs. It seemed like a logical step therefore that when the territories were reassigned in September, specialization by line of business be considered.

Rows Corporation had tried specialization in the past with partial success. Several years before, the company had requested that each branch assign their top salesperson to handle a particular product and call on several lines of business with standard packages. The results were that the salespeople found little demand for the product, but while faced with the prospective customer, presented the rest of the product line with quite a bit of success.

The size of the branch has a lot to do with product and line-of-business specialization. In large branches, one person is assigned Group V and VI responsibility for the entire branch, regardless of who handles the accounts for Groups I and II. In Portsmouth, this was considered impractical because of the specialized nature of the products and because there was no strong computer base with which to sell terminals. Portsmouth was primarily a Group I and II branch with some Group III, V, VI, and VIII quota.

The management of the Portsmouth branch weighed the following advantages and disadvantages to line-of-business specialization before revising the territory structure in 1976.

Advantages
1. Better utilization of standard packages because of salespeople's knowledge of them.
2. More complete knowledge in salespeople's selected accounts.
3. Customers seem to enjoy being called on by a specialist.
4. Salesperson should be able to make faster installations, thereby increasing productivity.
5. Salesperson will have more complete control of territory.
6. Salesperson will be able to use existing installations as sales tools in like accounts.
7. Many types of accounts, such as credit unions, are a very close-knit group. If salesperson can sell one in group, others will follow.
8. Rows' most successful competitor sells this way.

Disadvantages
1. Increased expenses. Specialists will have to cover six-county area instead of just one.
2. Younger salespeople would not learn all systems which they should know if they desire a management position.
3. It would be very difficult to cover all lines of business with only six men.
4. Some parts of branch territory, such as Barry County, do not have enough prospects to justify sending a specialist. It would be foolish to send a person fifty miles to make one call.

Summary

Each of the 249 Rows branches around the country were faced with a rapidly changing marketplace and product line. Various branch offices had already taken steps to meet assigned quotas that could exceed $3,000,000 in Group I, II, VI, and VIII alone.

The most popular means of solving the problem was line-of-business specialization. Most branches had at least one specialist and sometimes two of them. This was a by-product of the company's previous attempt at product specialization by line of business. Several branches, however, including Akron, had assigned all of their salespeople line-of-business responsibility along with a small geographic territory.

Portsmouth, with a quota of $1,500,000, was one of the smaller branches in terms of quota, but one of the larger in terms of geographic territory.

The assigning of small geographic territories along with line-of-business specialization appealed to the management of Portsmouth, because this approach seems to overcome many of the disadvantages mentioned earlier. They also thought that they could operate efficiently with only a partial specialization of their sales force. This would enable them to put newer people into a geographic territory where they could become familiar with many different types of systems—a familiarity needed for future management responsibilities—and, at the same time, give them the goal of trying to get the specialist contract during the interim.

This would be the first major change in the marketing procedure in Portsmouth since the late 1950s and would have a powerful impact on the success of the branch and its management team during the coming years.

Exhibit 5   *Estimated contribution of lines of business to total branch sales*

1. Over 10 percent contribution:
    A. Governmental units — schools, cities, counties
    B. Financial institutions — banks and savings and loan associations
2. Over 5 percent contribution:
    A. Auto dealers
    B. Credit unions
    C. Fuel-oil dealers
    D. Hospitals
    E. Accountants
    F. Contractors

The above figures vary by branch and during given years. However, it was felt that in Portsmouth, the strongest base for new business was in governmental and financial accounts.

The new Series L had caused an increasing shift in emphasis from manufacturing to retail and wholesale billing with sales analysis. It was expected that this type of system would contribute a greater share to branch sales in the future than it had in the past.

The branch manager has been concerned with the following questions and their interrelationships.

1. What is meant by the term 'software'?
    Software is the program(s) required to perform various functions on a "soft" computer — that is, one that has no mechanical linkage. All third-generation equipment (computers using microminiature components) is "soft."
2. What is meant by the term "downtime?"
    Downtime is that time that equipment is not running due to mechanical or electrical failure.

3. Since Groups V, VI, and VIII are new, will there be increased emphasis on these products?

   Quotas will continue to grow for these products until eventually they will make up the largest segment of the product line. Many of these units are specialized in nature and would be handled by one of the specialists. This may be an indirect advantage to the specialist program in that business is generated for these products without product specialization.

4. Are some of the mechanical models becoming obsolete?

   The Series J, P, F, and E equipment is being phased out and being replaced by electronic calculators and the Series L mini-computer. With the exception of some specialty products, the Group I and II line will eventually consist only of the above two product lines.

5. Would specialists carry higher quotas?

   Probably, because of the increase in sales this program would hopefully generate. However, it is doubtful that they would increase in proportion to the potential this contract would offer.

6. Could commission rates change?

   Management at this time does not foresee a change in the commission structure for specialists. It is hoped that a specialist's contract is one that only a superior salesperson could obtain and would be a target for the newer people.

7. Is partial specialization possible?

   Yes, many branches have already instituted variations to the program. It is, however, felt by Portsmouth's management that if a person is made a specialist, she or he should handle all like accounts within the branch. Some branches have specialists that handle lines of business in three counties, but all others in the branch are handled by the territory people. Portsmouth did not think this approach was practical, because it defeats many advantages of the program.

8. What would happen if the change was not made, and all salespeople handled geographic territories?

   Experience with the new products in 1975 and 1976 had convinced management that the branch's objectives could not be met continuing the status quo.

Questions

Is product specialization the best basis for Rows to organize its sales force?

What other alternatives does it have?

chapter

9

Price Cases

HERSHEL ELECTRONICS
Private vs National Brands

The Hershel Electronics Company was formed in 1940 by Robert Cohen. Mr. Cohen, in his youth, was very interested in electronics. He had no formal education in this field, but his intense interest developed into a working knowledge on the subject. He started a small company when he was still young by collecting and then selling small electronic components such as resistors and transistors. Most of what he sold was surplus equipment that he could pick up cheap, work on himself, and then resell.

Mr. Cohen did very well selling these surplus parts and opened his own store in St. Louis. While it first started out with just the surplus supplies, the store soon began to carry radios, televisions, and other related electronic components. The store grew steadily until, in 1976, the Hershel Electronics Company owned and operated five stores in the St. Louis area.

Hershel Electronics now deals more with the selling of stereos, radios, tape recorders, television antennas, and television tubes than with surplus parts. Hershel's sells all name-brand merchandise. The company has franchises with Panasonic, Sony, Concord, Ampex, Scott, Fisher, and other big name companies. The company still sells surplus parts, but the percentage of total sales for this area is quite small.

Although Hershel's sells tape recorders, stereos, televisions, and radios, most of the company's income comes from the sales of television antennas and tubes. There are two reasons for this. First of all, the markup on both items is well above the markup set on the other items that Hershel sells. Hershel's makes up

Submitted by Thomas R. Hart

to a 50 percent gross margin on tubes and even more on antennas. Hershel's also still shows a good profit on the surplus items sold.

Robert Cohen is still the major owner and manages the main store. He has hired another person to do the purchasing for the stores and to organize the company. Each store has a manager over a number of salespeople. Salespeople are paid strictly on an hourly basis, unless they have been with the firm for a considerable time; then they are on salary. No one works on a commission basis.

The company also employs antenna installation people. The installation staff works through the store, but independent of the store. Hershel's sells antennas either in kits—for the buyer to put up—or as a package deal, including installation. There is a flat rate of $25 for installation and this amount is paid to the installation people for their services. Although Hershel's makes no extra profit by selling antennas with installation, they have found that having this service available to their customers increases their sales of antennas.

Hershel's also makes available a rather unique service of having their salespeople trained and available to check customers' tubes in the store, free of charge. This gives the customer confidence that the equipment is being checked by someone who is qualified. Although this service does take up quite a bit of the salespeople's time, it does give Hershel's two important advantages over similar stores with do-it-yourself testers. First, it attracts a lot of customers who do not have the time or the desire to test their own tubes. Customers who do come in for this service have a habit of coming back again. Secondly, because the tubes are tested at Hershel's, the customers replace any bad tubes at the store. This contributes greatly to tube sales. Another factor is that while people are having their tubes checked, they have a tendency to wander around the store and purchase other items.

Although Hershel stores are not the most attractive stores around, they do make up for the lack of eye appeal in service and in the stock of national brands.

Hershel's had done a good but modest business until 1976, when Olsen Electronics came on the scene. Olsen's is a much larger, nationwide company that sells much the same products as Hershels.

Unlike Hershel's, Olsen does not carry the big brand names but puts its own name on radios and stereos. The production and selling of its brand allows Olsen to underprice Hershel's on comparable items. Hershel's can not sell the national brands for lower prices, because the prices were set by the companies themselves. If they were to sell them cheaper they could lose their franchise. On the other hand, many people were willing to pay more for an established name on the product.

In three instances, Olsen stores have moved in within a block or two of Hershel stores. Within two years, two of Hershel's stores closed down. The rest remain in operation. Mr. Cohen has tried several approaches to make his stores more competitive, including increased advertising, cost cutting through reducing services and improved warranties. Mr. Cohen is beginning to think that prices are the key to his problem.

Questions

Can Hershel use its brand and therefore reduce prices?
What other possibilities for lowering price does Mr. Cohen have?
Is price the problem?

WORLD WIDE TELEVISION AND APPLIANCES COMPANY
Interacting Factors Affecting Price

During the past week, the World Wide Television and Appliance Company, located on the northwest side of Detroit, Michigan, had been introduced to a new model of Arctic refrigerators, which they are currently selling.

Mr. Normal Paulson, who is the owner of the store, established the company during the summer of 1956. Before this establishment, Mr. Paulson was a salesperson, along with Mr. Burton and Mrs. Jevyak, for S. S. Houff Television and Appliances in Detroit. Upon the closing of this store, these three people decided to go into business for themselves. So it was during the summer of 1956 that Mr. Burton and Mrs. Jevyak went to work under Mr. Paulson's supervision.

The three started off very small by repairing televisions. Soon they decided to add retail sales of new televisions, stereos, and radios to their line of services. This expansion included all models of RCA and Zenith. They grew larger by selling large appliances. In 1962, they had to buy a larger store and warehouse and add more people to their staff. Currently, World Wide employs five salespeople, seven servicepeople, and one secretary. Since the novelty of having a new store wore off in 1964, business has settled down to a constant level.

Buyers of World Wide products are public establishments and individual families. The public establishments include restaurants, taverns, hospitals, churches, colleges, schools, and funeral homes. Basically, however, most of World Wide's sales are credited to individual families.

Submitted by Wayne Piotrowski

The new model TWE71MP Arctic refrigerator has modern lines styled by one of the country's leading designers. It is the newest of the Arctic line. The TWE71MP model comes in six colors.

The price of Model TWE71MP refrigerator will be marked after it arrives at the store, but as with all goods acquired by retailers, prices should be determined before the goods are purchased. There is nothing to prevent World Wide from offering Model TWE71MP at any price they desire, but this may result in little or no profit, whether the price is too high or too low. There is no simple formula World Wide can use when making pricing decisions, because many interacting factors require consideration, and their importance varies with each pricing problem.

Before deciding to market their new Arctic refrigerator, World Wide Television and Appliance—in cooperation with two sections of the city of Detroit in which a majority of their customers live — conducted a market trial. These sections were divided by zip codes. The zip codes 48223 and 48219 were the two areas selected. The primary objective of the two-section city test was to determine the relative marketability of the TWE71MP model Arctic refrigerator under two different premium rate plans. One plan consisted of a high initial price charged only once, while the other consisted of a lower initial charge with monthly payments. These rate structures provided the same rate of return in the long run.

World Wide had two other objectives that were under consideration when this new model refrigerator was introduced. First of all, they wanted to determine the effect this new refrigerator would have on families in each of the two areas of Detroit under each pricing policy. Secondly, they wanted to determine what features of this model attracted the customers.

These objectives were accomplished by a controlled test consisting of a random sample of the market and by a survey. As a sales test, salespeople used every fifth television buyer until 123 customers had been tested for the sample. Every other day, the sales personnel tried to sell their customers the TWE71MP Arctic refrigerator at the large initial price to customers of the 48219 area, while on the alternate days they tried to sell this refrigerator to the 48223 market at the installment price in which the charges could be paid over a period from three to twelve months.

The test results based on the customers who returned within the year to purchase a refrigerator were summarized in terms of total refrigerators sold. Exhibit 1 illustrates the results.

Exhibit 2 shows a few comparisons between the installment plan and the "pay once" plan. As indicated by this exhibit, 85

Exhibit 1   *Preferred payment plan by actual sales*

Model TWE71MP Arctic refrigerator Installment plan (48223)   22%
Model TWE71MP Arctic refrigerator One-payment plan (48219)   8%
All other Arctic refrigerators sold (all Detroit)   70%
                                                              ―――――
                                                               100%

percent of those who bought the refrigerator on the installment plan believed that they were getting their money's worth as compared to the 73 percent on the one-payment plan. The test indicates that 22 percent of the installment-plan customers bought refrigerators out of the total number of customers approached, while only 8 percent of the one-payment-plan customers bought one. And 55 percent of the installment-plan customers felt that the level of rate was fair as compared to only 24 percent of the one-payment-plan customers.

In gathering information by the use of a survey, World Wide was interested in determining which special features attracted

Exhibit 2   *Reason payment plan preferred*

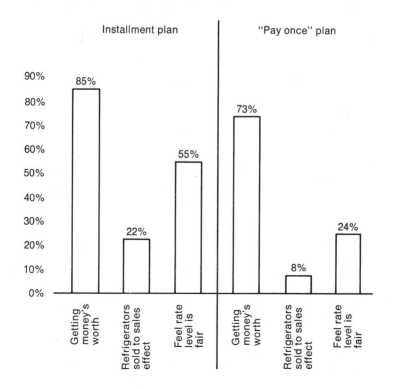

potential customers and some characteristics of the refrigerator buyers.

The reactions to the features of model TWE71MP are illustrated in Exhibit 3.

Exhibit 3   *Reaction to product characteristics.*

| | Reactions | |
Refrigerator characteristics	Favorable	Unfavorable
Size 17.1 cubic feet	38%	62%
Shape and style	42	58
Color	89	11
Ice maker	20	80
Freezer space	35	65
Good service	37	63

The characteristics of the actual model TWE71MP refrigerator purchasers can be seen in Exhibit 4.

Exhibit 4   *Demographics of purchasers by payment plan selected*

	Installment plan 48223	"Pay once" plan 48219
Socioeconomic class		
Upper class	0%	0%
Lower-upper class	4%	27%
Upper-middle class	25%	35%
Lower-middle class	61%	35%
Upper-lower class	10%	3%
Lower class	0%	0%
Total	100%	100%
Age		
Under 35	39%	41%
35 – 55	42%	53%
Over 55	19%	6%
Total	100%	100%
Marital status		
Single	5%	3%
Married – no children	26%	30%
Married – small children	41%	29%
Married – adult children	28%	38%
Total	100%	100%
Housing		
Own home	76%	56%
Rent	18%	15%
Other	6%	29%
Total	100%	100%

From the total 123 interviews completed from the two zip code areas, the results in Exhibit 4 were based on the salespeople's judgment. World Wide would like to use this and other information that might be needed to set up a pricing system and procedure.

Questions

Set up a pricing system for World Wide using the information they have obtained. Justify your system.

What are the interacting factors which affect price?

HONES INDUSTRIES
Industrial Price

Company Background

Hones Industries, Inc., is a small privately owned corporation engaged in the production and distribution of standardized industrial parts for large national manufacturers. Their products include standard nipples and hose fittings, shoulders and outer races for bearings, and various similar products. Buyers for these products included Aeroquip, Inc., Clark Equipment, and Hoover Ball Bearing.

Hones Industries was founded in 1967 by Robert Hones, Ruth Wynn, and Leo Miller. Hones was a recent business graduate of the University of California. Wynn, a friend of Hones, had experience in management and production of standardized parts. Miller was the owner of the building and facilities. Miller owned several small machine shops in the area, but these shops produced parts not related to the products of Hones Industries. Miller agreed to form a corporation with Hones and Wynn. It was agreed that Hones and Wynn would actively run the business, with Miller serving as an inactive partner.

Hones Industries started in 1967 as a one-plant operation. The building was new with 9,000 square feet of work space, excluding the office and washroom. Capital equipment included six Acme automatic screw machines, three Warner and Swasey turret lathes, one drill press, and a centrifugal spin tub for shavings. Total capital investment in 1967 was approximately $2 million. Of the

Submitted by David C. Torey

total investment, $50,000 was put in by each of the three owners. The other $1,850,000 was secured through loans at 6 percent interest. $850,000 would be paid off during the next ten years. A million would have to be refinanced at the end of ten years. Sales for 1967 were $350,000. This figure was a normal volume for firms of this size in the industry. All sales were made to three customers: Aeroquip, Clark, and Hoover. These firms remain Hones' chief customers, accounting for 95 percent of sales annually.

In 1973, Hones Industries decided to purchase additional equipment. Two new Acme automatic screw machines were purchased, valued at $250,000 each. One new Warner and Swasey lathe was purchased, valued at $60,000. Twenty-five percent of this amount was paid in cash. The balance was financed through a local bank on a five-year loan. With a favorable cash position and sunny sales forecasts, Hones Industries appeared to be in good financial condition.

In 1974 and 1975, Hones Industries enjoyed a sales volume 10 percent above the industry average and decided to expand facilities. A small shop was purchased nearby, with 2,500 square feet of floor space. Two automatic screw machines and one lathe were already in the shop and were purchased along with the building and the land. These facilities were purchased for $300,000, financed by a ten-year loan. The equipment and building were considered to have a life expectancy of twenty-five years.

Since its beginning in 1967, Hones Industries had established itself as a quality producer of standardized parts. This was supported by consistently rising sales volumes annually. In 1975, sales volume was $525,000.

Industry Background

The industry for standard industrial parts is large and complex. In the specific types of products that Hones Industries sells, the market is dominated by four large national firms, with many smaller firms also represented. The four large companies account for about 85 percent of total industry sales. However, buyers for these products sometimes favor the smaller suppliers for emergency orders because of their convenient locations.

The industry as a whole has been very competitive. Prices, quality, and service are virtually the same for most of the firms. Buyers in this market for standard parts demand certain product characteristics and delivery requirements which had to be adhered to. Product differentiation has no place here. Recently, however, the picture had changed; buyers were scrambling for sources of supply, as was Hones. From one day to the next, it was difficult to know whether raw materials would be available. The upward changes in prices were fantastic.

Hones Industries' Market Picture

Hones Industries' forecast for 1976 predicted sales of approximately $535,000, a 2 percent increase over 1975. The recent developments in the industry, however, cast some doubt on the validity of this forecast.

Most recently, a price hike for a raw material had been initiated by one of the large suppliers, and the others were sure to follow. The price amounted to a 10 percent average increase in the material purchased by Hones Industries. The price hike was the third "announced" hike of the year. Even with the increased price, the suppliers could not always deliver. They refused to draw up any contracts on price and delivery quantities and preferred to take care of their large purchasers first.

The present conditions became apparent about eight months ago. If they continue they may have the effect of weeding out a number of the smaller suppliers like Hones.

Continued price hikes and a material shortage would severely affect Hones Industries. The break-even point was higher for this firm than for the big firms because it did not enjoy the economies of scale resulting from high-volume production. Also, the capital loans were a concern; they had to be refinanced shortly.

Two of Hones' customers had recently sent contracts for annual supplies. One contract called for $200,000 of merchandise, the other $300,000. Both contracts offered a large increase in price: 15 percent. The correspondence from both companies had indicated that they were going to insure the products they needed by contract for the next year. If Hones would not or could not, the customer would go to someone else and get a contract, even if the terms were less favorable. Hones' management, under ordinary conditions, would have been eager to sign the contract; but these were not ordinary times—with increasing cost, short supply, and the like.

Questions

Should Hones accept the contracts at the 15 percent price increase?
Would price indexing work for them?
Devise a plan of action for Hones' management.

GERBER PRODUCTS COMPANY
Gaining Acceptance
of and with a Price Cut

Situation

In December of 1970, Fred Yeakey, vice-president of marketing for Gerber Products Company, was considering a proposal to reduce the selling price per jar of canned baby food and to promote the line aggressively. The objectives of the proposal were reducing the price per jar at the retail level and the entire project was aimed at the New York City market only.

To accomplish these objectives, the proposal called for a sales development allowance campaign whereby the retailer could buy the canned baby food at a reduced price per jar and sell to the consumer at a lower price per jar, in addition earning a profit of 50 percent more on each jar they sold. It was hoped that this reduced price would stimulate retailers to buy more Gerber canned baby food and enable Gerber to realize a larger share of the New York City market.

Marketing Opportunities

Although the birth rate (births per thousand population) remains relatively stable, the number of births is increasing moderately and a substantial increase is expected by 1980. Population control, especially as it affects our environment, is very much a topic of discussion for Gerber. As a company specializing in baby needs and services, the market is, of course, tied closely to the number

---

While the case is a portrayal of conditions and decisions made in 1970, it no longer reflects the conditions, decisions, or operating philosophy of Gerbers.

of births throughout the world. With more women in the prime child-bearing age group and an increase in the consumption of baby food per baby, there are certainly additional opportunities for Gerber growth within their rather specialized market.

Early in the spring of 1970 a new television theme was introduced in selected prime-market areas. A modern musical number was especially adapted for Gerber use and has proved to have a unique appeal to the young-mother audience for which it is intended.

New marketing opportunities could also be seen through the growth of United States grocery sales. Moving up year by year, United States grocery sales were expected to hit an estimated $86.8 billion in 1971, rising 12 percent to $97.3 billion by 1975, according to the Jansen Retail Index. Frank Graf, executive vice-president of P.L. Jansen Co., said that higher food sales and fewer stores would call for changing marketing plans by food advertisers.

The Competitive Situation

Most producers of canned baby food produce only under their own label. Most larger brands are sold widely over broad regions for the United States, and Gerber also produces and sells in the European market. In 1971, Gerber was the leading producer of baby food, having 60 percent of the total market. Lunt maintained 20 percent of the total market and Wheeler was close behind them.

Gerber and Lunt both offer their products in a choice of strained or junior-sized. Baby food production is very closely watched and regulated to insure consumers of the highest possible quality for their babies' needs.

The industry outlook for the future was excellent, since the food and grocery field was the nation's largest retail market. Food stores account for about one-fifth to one-fourth of United States retail sales. But, with grocery sales nearing $87 billion in 1971 and expected to exceed $97 billion in 1975, the industry was doing more than merely keeping up with the population growth.

Food marketing has been getting faster and more efficient. Food companies that were testing new products for six to twelve months in large test markets more recently were getting similar results in half the time.

Advertising in the baby food industry is usually limited to women's magazines that stress care of the baby. Gerber sends out many journals that are directed to the new mothers, describing every aspect of child care. Spot television commercials are also widely used in morning and afternoon shows where the mother-and-child audience is greatest.

Gerber distributes its products exclusively through its own sales force, but many of the smaller producers rely on food brokers who are allowed some freedom in negotiating price.

The Proposal

The proposal Mr. Yeakey was considering dealt only with the New York City market. The city of New York represented approximately 10 percent of the nation's baby food business. Gerber total national share of the baby food market in 1970 was about 60 percent, but in New York City it was only 25 percent, while Lunt had 64 percent, Wheeler 6 percent, and Goodwin and Company 5 percent.

In the past, Gerber had tried many innovations to capture a larger share of the New York City market. Among these were radio, television, newspaper, and direct-mail promotions—all of which were of little success. These past promotions failed because they could not get trade acceptance. They had consumer acceptance, but without stores providing Gerber with more shelf space, they just could not crack the New York City area.

Gerber was prepared to approach the New York City market with their Sales Development Allowance (SDA) program, even though the Lunt Company had tried a similar program recently and was unsuccessful. Gerber felt that this program would be successful for them because unlike the Lunt Company, they had consumer acceptance.

At the time this program was considered, Gerber was offering baby food to the retailer on the basis of $.10 per jar and the retailers were selling it at $.12 a jar or making a profit of $.02 per jar. Under the SDA program, Gerber would offer the baby food at $.08 per jar and suggest that the retailer sell at $.11 per jar. Here the retailer's costs are $.02 less per jar and their profit 50 percent more.

An important consideration was that, by reducing the selling price, Gerber was not risking as much money as Lunt did when they attempted a similar project. For Lunt to meet Gerber's price, it cost them much more, since Lunt had 64 percent of the market and Gerber only 25 percent. The cost of the project to Gerber would be low since the profits derived from the increased sales could offset the SDA project.

Questions

Should Gerber go ahead with the SDA program in order to gain a larger share of the New York market? Justify your answer.

How else might Gerber use price to gain a greater share of the New York market?

chapter ─────────────── 10

Marketing Evaluation
Measurements Cases

WESTERN SPORTS INCORPORATED
Evaluating Sales Districts

In the summer of 1971, Mr. Harold Johnson, recently appointed Vice-President in charge of sales of Western Sports Incorporated (WSI), was concerned about the company's sales trend in its fifth district. The fifth district is comprised of Michigan, Indiana, Pennsylvania, Ohio and Wisconsin. The company's other four districts were generating an increasing total sales figure on a continuous basis. Although, as a whole, WSI was showing an annual sales

Exhibit 1   *States comprising the five districts*

District I
  California
  Oregon
  Washington
  Idaho
  Montana
District II
  Wyoming
  Colorado
  Arizona
  New Mexico
  Utah
District III
  North Dakota
  South Dakota
  Nebraska
  Minnesota
  Iowa

District IV
  Oklahoma
  Kansas
  Missouri
  Illinois
  Texas
District V
  Michigan
  Indiana
  Ohio
  Pennsylvania
  Wisconsin

Submitted by James F. Van Dam, Law Student, Cooley Law School

increase, Mr. Johnson felt that the fifth district could equal or match any of the other four districts in total sales. He decided to review the fifth district and its success in meeting the competition of other sporting goods manufacturers selling within this five-state area. He also considered whether a change in distribution and/or pricing policies would be beneficial in increasing total sales volume in district five. Mr. Johnson wondered whether the trend in district five could affect the sales in other districts.

The Firm

In 1930, WSI established its sporting goods manufacturing firm in Sacramento, California. By the beginning of 1940, the firm had a total of five different manufacturing sites. They are Sacramento, California; Phoenix, Arizona; Minneapolis, Minnesota; Grand Rapids, Michigan; and St. Louis, Missouri. Each of the additional four plants had been former competitors of Western. WSI purchased each business to facilitate growth in these new areas and reduce the transportation costs of finished goods distribution. (Previously WSI had been producing sporting goods manufactured in the Sacramento plant and distributing them to retailers throughout the five districts.) Currently, each district is operated as a separate entity with each manufacturing plant being the central headquarters for its own district. The home office remains in Sacramento, and it is here that district performance is analyzed and evaluated in terms of (1) past history and (2) comparison to other districts.

Sporting Goods

WSI manufactures eight different lines of sporting goods. These range from baseballs to bowling balls. Because WSI's policy has always been to sell sporting goods that far surpass the official sporting rule book's specifications on quality, their products have been widely used by many professional and semiprofessional sports organizations (such as the National and American baseball, football, and basketball leagues.) With professionals using Western's products, Western has been able to build an image of quality in the market for their products. Many promotional campaigns have been organized around a popular professional athlete's endorsement of a particular WSI product. This has aided the firm's market standing among amateur users, who make up approximately 85 percent of WSI's total end sales (approximately 15 percent of sales are to professional and semiprofessional sports organizations).

Exhibit 2

Sales per district of eight WSI products, 1970-75

Year	Base-balls	Foot-balls	Basket-balls	Soccer balls	Tennis balls	Bowling balls	Golf balls	Hand balls	District
1970	60,000	54,800	31,300	2,800	31,000	14,000	29,000	4,200	District I
1971	76,400	59,500	39,600	4,700	39,600	18,600	31,200	6,500	
1972	69,600	68,300	39,900	10,900	47,200	21,400	39,600	11,400	
1973	78,300	74,700	45,800	12,700	48,100	31,100	47,400	14,800	
1974	84,200	79,000	51,200	13,800	55,300	31,600	49,300	18,600	
1975	91,000	31,600	59,700	15,000	69,000	31,800	57,600	19,400	
1970	54,000	39,400	31,700	3,900	35,000	19,500	27,300	4,900	District II
1971	63,000	47,300	35,200	4,600	39,600	21,300	28,200	4,700	
1972	71,400	49,900	39,600	9,100	41,700	30,100	41,000	10,600	
1973	79,600	56,700	43,400	14,600	49,600	32,000	47,400	11,400	
1974	81,200	61,300	49,900	19,300	60,700	34,700	51,300	15,300	
1975	86,000	68,000	58,400	26,900	71,000	35,300	59,400	20,100	
1970	67,000	41,600	33,000	4,100	39,000	19,300	21,300	4,100	District III
1971	69,700	50,600	35,000	4,600	39,000	20,300	22,400	4,900	
1972	80,100	51,900	39,700	9,100	47,300	29,600	41,700	5,700	
1973	84,000	63,200	46,300	10,900	59,400	31,300	49,600	7,300	
1974	91,300	69,100	49,100	12,400	71,200	33,300	51,900	9,100	
1975	98,300	71,300	59,600	17,000	84,000	39,000	60,400	16,000	
1970	57,000	61,000	31,000	3,700	27,300	14,400	22,600	3,900	District IV
1971	69,400	63,300	39,300	4,700	29,200	15,400	29,600	4,600	
1972	71,300	65,000	41,700	9,100	47,000	19,200	41,200	4,700	
1973	76,000	71,000	43,200	10,600	49,400	31,400	47,600	9,600	
1974	79,000	72,400	47,600	14,300	51,200	39,700	49,000	14,300	
1975	89,000	74,000	48,000	15,900	59,600	46,000	59,600	19,700	
1970	59,400	47,000	39,000	3,300	29,700	15,800	25,400	4,200	District V
1971	47,100	39,600	29,900	2,700	21,000	14,300	19,600	3,600	
1972	46,400	38,400	19,600	1,900	19,600	12,200	15,200	2,500	
1973	39,300	35,000	14,400	2,100	19,300	11,700	14,900	1,900	
1974	37,900	34,300	14,600	2,000	17,900	10,400	13,800	1,800	
1975	35,900	49,900	13,400	1,900	16,800	9,600	12,700	1,800	

The Research and Development Department of WSI had been recently attempting to expand the product line offered. Top management has also suggested developing two separate quality products to gain a larger share of the market. These projects are now in the innovative stages of development.

Distribution and Pricing

Distribution at WSI is directly from the manufacturing plant to the retail outlet or sports organization. Each district has one district manager with one senior salesperson and junior salesperson per state. The salesforce calls on prospective buyers who are order-takers from established accounts within their state. Most salespeople have their own office staff within their state that can take telephone orders from customers or can help with customer problems. This sales office staff also facilitates the product flow from manufacturer to consumer. The follow-up procedure is to give prompt and efficient delivery and to insure customer satisfaction. The function of the typical sales office staff as a distributive link is shown more clearly in Exhibit 3. Once the orders have been made through the salesperson to the manufacturing plant, the goods are delivered by a truck-transport network that operates from the central office in each district. Delivery time is usually ten days or less from the date the order is placed.

The pricing policy is determined by the district's central office. The mark-up normally fluctuates from 10 to 20 percent for the products sold. Prices are occasionally adjusted to meet the prices of competitive sporting goods of similar quality.

As mentioned earlier, WSI sold goods to retail outlets at a 10-20 percent mark-up on gross cost of goods with a 5-15 percent net profit on sales. The retailers in turn have a mark-up on the items that they sold. The athletic association usually paid 3-5 percent more for goods than the retailers. The credit terms offered by the manufacturer are 1/10/n30. There is no shipping charge; this cost was absorbed by WSI.

The Fifth District

The fifth district's sales manager is Mr. Peter Kroeshell. Mr. Kroeshell has been with the firm since 1948, when he began as a junior salesperson. His responsibility as sales manager is to insure good selling practices (according to company policy) and to see that his sales force is adequately covering their market. The district's research and development projects, on a monthly basis, a sales

Exhibit 3   *Function and organization chart*

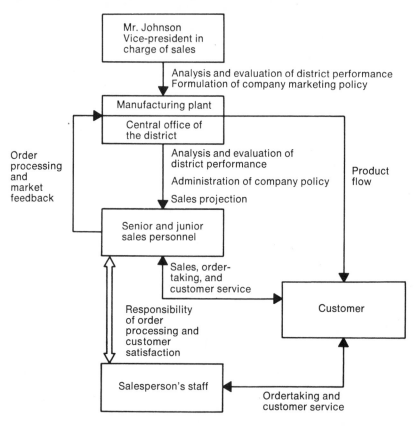

forecast for each person's territory. This forecast is accomplished with the assistance of the salesperson involved. Through this person's feedback on market changes, top management attempts to gain a more precise insight into shifts in demand.

In this district, the average senior salesperson's salary is $15,000 per year and the average junior salesperson's salary is $9,500 per year. They each receive one-half of 1 percent on their total dollar sales, plus liberal expense accounts. The senior sales force is made up of people whose years of service with WSI range from fifteen to thirty years. The greatest percentage of their accounts have been developed by their hard work and have been standing accounts for many years. The five junior salespeople in the fifth district have been with the firm for an average of four years. Many of their accounts have been taken over from the senior salesperson (the result of the territory becoming too large for one person to cover). Because of the high-caliber sales personnel recruited by WSI, the attrition rate is extremely low. Due to a record of top-quality products and excellent service, WSI salespeople have an

Exhibit 4 Customer types and percent of sales in WSI's fifth district

Customer categories	Percent of total sales					
	1970	1971	1972	1973	1974	1975
Hardware stores	8%	8%	7%	4%	4%	4%
Discount stores	2%	3%	3%	4%	4%	3%
Athletic organizations	14%	16%	12%	15%	14%	15%
Sports shops	6%	12%	12%	13%	14%	14%
Chain department stores	65%	55%	50%	49%	49%	48%
Independent department stores	5%	6%	16%	15%	15%	16%
Total	100%	100%	100%	100%	100%	100%

Sales (in dollars) of chain department store accounts in District 5 (1970–75)

Customer accounts	Sales in dollars					
	1970	1971	1972	1973	1974	1975
Sears, Roebuck and Company	4,700,000	3,900,000	3,000,000	2,200,000	1,900,000	1,600,000
Montgomery Ward Company	3,200,000	2,700,000	2,200,000	1,800,000	1,500,000	1,300,000
W. T. Grant Company	1,000,000	1,100,000	1,100,000	1,300,000	1,400,000	1,400,000
J. C. Penney Company	800,000	850,000	850,000	875,000	900,000	900,000
All others	900,000	900,000	950,000	100,000	150,000	1,100,000

outstanding working relationship with many of their customers. Each customer is called on at least once a month with large accounts called on as often as once a week.

The retail outlets vary from small hardware stores to some of the largest chain stores in the United States. The chain department stores are some of the largest accounts that WSI has on the books. Four of the largest buyers are Sears, Roebuck and Company, Montgomery Ward and Company, W. T. Grant Company, and J. C. Penney Company. For a breakdown of customer types and major accounts, see Exhibit 4. Two of these accounts (Sears and Wards) were WSI's largest customers in 1970. Late in that year, however, they began producing their own sporting goods that were competitive with WSI's products. Both of these firms have decided to produce sporting goods for their department stores on a limited basis. They have sold their own manufactured sport products east of Chicago from 1970 through 1975. According to informed sources, they planned in 1970 to expand their production to cover the entire United States market, if the first five years were successful.

Competition and the Future

Mr. Johnson was concerned over the tremendous drop in sales due to Sears' and Wards' sporting goods production. He also anticipated the possibility of a reduction in sales in the other districts due to the expected expansion. This fear was based on the high level of purchases made by these and other chain department stores in the other four districts. Because the general distribution of customer types was similar throughout WSI's districts, the new sporting goods producers could do great harm to WSI's total sales volume.

Some Alternatives Considered
1. Wholesale trade as middleman. For the last two years, both Rogers Wholesalers, Inc., and B. P. Distributors have been attempting to take on the WSI line of sporting goods. Each of these firms are national chain wholesalers and insist they could increase market coverage and total sales of the Western line. The plans offered by Rogers and B. P. were very similar. They would purchase WSI's sporting goods at 5 to 7 percent below the prices retail outlets were now paying. They offered the following advantages:

Exhibit 5   *Sales mix*

Sales to customer categories
(in number of items sold)

Customer categories	1970	1971	1972	1973	1974	1975
District I						
Hardware stores	41,000	46,000	49,000	42,000	46,000	41,000
Discount stores	11,000	12,000	15,000	17,000	19,000	26,000
Athletic organizations	50,000	56,000	47,000	49,000	49,000	56,000
Sports shops	30,000	40,000	47,000	51,000	54,000	57,000
Chain department stores	87,000	90,000	91,000	94,000	96,000	111,000
Independent						
department stores	32,000	47,000	49,000	61,000	67,000	69,000
District II						
Hardware stores	36,000	37,000	37,000	45,000	48,000	46,000
Discount stores	14,000	15,000	16,000	19,000	26,000	29,000
Athletic organizations	52,000	53,000	54,000	58,000	59,000	65,000
Sports shops	37,000	41,000	56,000	59,000	94,000	73,000
Chain department stores	69,000	71,000	78,000	91,000	98,000	102,000
Independent						
department stores	31,000	30,000	37,000	39,000	35,000	42,000
District III						
Hardware stores	31,000	36,000	36,000	39,000	47,000	47,000
Discount stores	19,000	21,000	29,000	34,000	36,000	39,000
Athletic organizations	51,000	50,000	54,000	55,000	59,000	61,000
Sport shops	30,000	34,000	39,000	47,000	50,000	51,000
Chain department stores	78,000	84,000	89,000	94,000	97,000	103,000
Independent						
department stores	31,000	34,000	37,000	34,000	41,000	42,000
District VI						
Hardware stores	27,000	29,000	41,000	46,000	46,000	46,000
Discount stores	16,000	21,000	23,000	29,000	29,000	32,000
Athletic organizations	59,000	60,000	61,000	47,000	42,000	47,000
Sport shops	31,000	34,000	41,000	41,000	43,000	47,000
Chain department stores	79,000	81,000	88,000	89,000	95,000	99,000
Independent						
department stores	27,000	28,000	29,000	34,000	39,000	39,000

    a. Transport to retailers (This would reduce WSI's delivery costs which now totaled 5 percent of total sales.)

    b. Some degree of advertising and sales promotion of the WSI product (At this point, only the large retail chains offered any amount of advertising and promotion.)

2. Reduce prices and offer product at a lower price than competition.

3. Increase the sales force so as to increase the coverage of the market area. This alternative would break down the area of responsibility for each salesperson. This would increase the amount of time each salesperson could spend with a customer. Although this might produce some increase in total sales, it is questionable whether the increased profit could exceed the increased expense. There is also the problem of reducing the

Exhibit 6   Firms of similar sales volume and similar size to WSI, 1970–75

Firm name	Dollar sales					
	1970	1971	1972	1973	1974	1975
McKinsy, Inc.	62,400,000	62,900,000	67,000,000	69,300,000	67,000,000	69,900,000
LaVern and Son, Inc.	75,800,000	75,900,000	76,100,000	77,200,000	77,200,000	78,400,000
W. A. Nielson Co.	86,400,000	86,900,000	87,400,000	89,100,000	89,900,000	91,200,000
W. H. Rochester, Inc.*	67,900,000	65,700,000	63,200,000	69,900,000	76,000,000	76,800,000
Montery Sports, Co.	63,000,000	63,800,000	64,100,000	65,200,000	65,800,000	65,900,000
Western Sports, Inc.	75,000,000	77,200,000	78,100,000	79,900,000	79,800,000	79,800,000

*Since 1973 this firm has sold sporting goods through its own exclusive sports shops.

accounts and the income of the established area sales personnel.

4. Expand the firm's markets to include areas of the Eastern United States.

5. Establish WSI sporting goods shops that are exclusive merchants of the WSI products. (W. H. Rochester, Inc., a competing sporting goods manufacturing firm of similar size to WSI, developed an exclusive chain of dealers in 1973. Their degree of success has been quite substantial, according to some of WSI's retail customers and available statistical data.)

Questions

To what is the decline in the fifth district due — sales force, department chain store changes in operating policy, the economy, what? Justify your answer.

Establish a sales force evaluation system for Western. What are the most important factors?

If competition is the cause of the decline, which one of the alternatives suggested (or other possibilities) would be the best strategy to increase sales? Justify.

SCHNUK CLOTHING. INC,
The Promotion Program

Schnuk Clothing was organized in 1957 as a partnership between Norman and Esther Schnuk, husband and wife. It remained as a partnership until January, 1976, when Norman and his two sons, Bill and Jim, incorporated to form the present Schnuk Clothing, Inc. Being completely family owned and operated, the 150,000 shares (at $1 a share) were divided up equally among the three family shareholders. In 1957, when the partnership was established and the initial investment of building and inventory was made, there was only one other competing clothing store in the town of Sebewaing, Michigan.

Sebewaing is a small town located on the thumb of Michigan. Its population is about 2,200 people, with farming and light industry the main sources of income for the residents. With some of the best farmland in the United States, Sebewaing and its surrounding communities have been slowly growing in population.

Mr. Schnuk has built up a reliable, up-to-date men's store over the years. He has concentrated on keeping the proper style and quantity of inventory at all times, trying to please his old customers and trying to make new ones.

In the fall of 1964, Schnuk Clothing expanded to Gaylord, Michigan. This community was in many ways like the home store in Sebewaing. The Gaylord store was about the same size, with the people wanting about the same types of goods. Different from the Sebewaing store, Gaylord catered to the ski customers who are free-spending, vacationing people.

Submitted by Frank Hofmeister, Jr., Account Executive, Colle and McVoy Advertising Agency, Minneapolis

The competition in Gaylord was a little stronger than in Sebewaing, but Mr. Schnuk again built up a strong clientele that made the store the leader in the area. Total gross sales for 1965 (first full year of operation) was a little over $100,000, putting it over the Sebewaing store, doing about $93,000 gross sales. Again, as in Sebewaing, Mr. Schnuk relied on fine-quality goods and reliable service to the customer to build up a good reputation.

Seeing an opportunity to take advantage of another area of Michigan, in the spring of 1967, Mr. Schnuk opened up a men's shop in Bad Axe, Michigan. This location is about thirty miles from the home store in Sebewaing, which would allow Mr. Schnuk and his wife to manage both stores until their eldest son would take over as manager the coming year.

Bad Axe is the county seat for Huron County and is a little larger than either Sebewaing or Gaylord. There were already three men's clothing stores in Bad Axe, but Mr. Schnuk had the insight to recognize that Bad Axe is growing rapidly and is the only "big town" in the area (this area includes about a sixty-mile radius).

He went about setting up this store as he did the two previous ones. First, he rented and redecorated the store site, then developed a good opening and follow-up promotion campaign, stocked the store with good quality merchandise, and above all stood behind his goods with reliable service.

As was calculated by Mr. Schnuk, the Bad Axe store saw no profits for the first two years of operation. Finally, for the year 1970, the Bad Axe store showed a substantial profit and in 1971 was the leader in gross sales for the three stores with gross sales of slightly over $150,000. The other two stores also showed substantial gains at this time, with Gaylord running second.

Another store was added in the fall of 1976. The location of this store was Vasser, Michigan. The town is about the same size as Bad Axe, but Vasser is located within forty miles of two rather large metropolitan areas, Saginaw and Flint, Michigan. For the most part, the residents of Vasser and surrounding communities work in either Saginaw or Flint, and commute back and forth to work each day. These commuters tend to spend their money in the bigger cities, but Mr. Schnuk knew if he offered the people the right merchandise, he could gain their patronage in the future. Because Vasser had no men's clothing store at all, Schnuk Clothing, Inc., realized a potential market here and went about setting up a fourth store. They followed the same procedure for opening as was followed by the previous stores. Because of the short time period since opening, no figures are available, but all indications point to another successful store.

Early in 1975, a discount clothing chain store opened in both Sebewaing and Gaylord. Their merchandise was below Schnuk Clothing's standards but was not what you could call "junk." The discount chain didn't call themselves discount stores and advertised their products as top-quality. Their prices were on a much lower level than Schnuk could compete against. The store's appearance and layout were very attractive and this chain could afford professional window dressers that did tremendous work for the material provided. The chain also ran extensive advertising campaigns in local papers and provided extra promotional material when needed.

There is also a low-grade clothing store in Bad Axe that has been there since before Mr. Schnuk opened his store in that area. Its effect has never been noticed and would be virtually impossible to measure, because the store was established before Schnuk Clothing moved to that town.

Mr. Schnuk and sons began questioning their advertising and special promotion programs. Were they extensive enough to compete with the new chain stores in both Sebewaing and Gaylord? Are all potential new customers being exposed to a Schnuk Clothing ad? Can we compete with the chain store when it comes to sales and special promotion campaigns?

The advertising media available in both the Sebewaing and Gaylord areas are almost identical. Each town has its own weekly newspaper. There is also a county paper that comes out once every two weeks in each of the areas. The county paper contains mostly news items pertaining to the county's affairs. It also is an important advertising media for many of the area businesses. The coverage of these two papers is quite extensive and very beneficial.

Mr. Schnuk observed that from May 1975 to May 1976, the chain store ran almost twice as many advertisements of almost twice the size as what Schnuk Clothing did for the same time period. To go along with this, gross sales in both Sebewaing and Gaylord had remained almost the same last year. Mr. Schnuk also noticed that the number of people entering both stores had dropped off considerably. Whether this was due to the economic situation or the new competition was not known, but Mr. Schnuk and sons decided something should be done to find the reasons behind their recent decreases.

Schnuk Clothing, Inc., had to answer some searching questions before they could proceed with their intentions of expanding again. Is our merchandise over-priced given its quality? Is our selection of merchandise extensive enough? Is our service in the store competitive with the chain store? Is the store's appearance and layout conducive to comfortable shopping? Are customers happy in, general, with Schnuk Clothing facilities?

These questions could only be answered by the shopping public. Mr. Schnuk employed the services of a college student for three weeks in August, 1976. This student utilized his marketing research and marketing problems knowledge, along with Mr. Schnuk's knowledge of the business, and came up with a short questionnaire to be answered in personal interviews. Exhibit 7 shows the questionnaire used in both Sebewaing and Gaylord. The interviews were conducted on Wednesday afternoon and Friday afternoon and night. These were the two busiest times for both stores. At least thirty interviews were collected for each day which would represent about 40 percent of the people entering the store on these days.

Exhibit 7   *Survey questionnaire*

_____Male   _____Female

1. Do you live in town or are you from the surrounding area?
   - _____town
   - _____surrounding area
   - _____other
2. How often a week do you shop here?
   - _____1 time
   - _____2 times
   - _____3 times
   - _____more
   - _____less
3. Is the quality of the merchandise acceptable to your shopping habits?
   - _____yes
   - _____no
4. Is the price of the merchandise too high, too low, or just right when compared to its quality?
   - _____too high
   - _____too low
   - _____just right
5. Is the service here courteous and dependable?
   - _____all the time
   - _____never
   - _____sometimes
6. How did you hear about this store and location for the first time?
   - _____from friend
   - _____from advertisement
   - _____from past experience
   - _____only one in town
   - _____other

7. Is the store physically attractive?

    _____yes

    _____no

8. About what percentage of your men's clothing buying do you do here?

    _____0%

    _____1 – 25%

    _____26 – 50%

    _____51 – 75%

    _____76 – 100%

9. Why do you shop here?

THANK YOU

Exhibit 8 gives the results of the Sebewaing survey. The results from Gaylord were almost identical, with some minor differences not relevant to the case.

Exhibit 8   *Results of Sebewaing survey*

From the Sebewaing survey, they got a return of sixty questionnaires. Gaylord also had a 100 percent return with the results very comparable.

Sebewaing's results: 24 male and 36 female

Question 1:

    40 — town

    16 — surrounding area

    4 — other

Question 2:

    40 — 1 time

    3 — 2 times

    17 — less

Question 3:

    58 — yes

    2 — no

Question 4

    5 — too high

    2 — too low

    53 — just right

Question 5:

    56 — all the time

    4 — sometimes

Question 6:

    7 — from friend

    3 — from advertisement

    35 — from past experience

    3 — only one in town

    12 — other

Question 7:

    60 — yes

    0 — no

Question 8:

```
 3 — 0%
 8 — 1 – 25%
19 — 26 – 50%
24 — 51 – 75%
 6 — 76 – 100%
```

Question 9:

Many varied answers, but the two most frequent responses were "good quality" and "properly priced merchandise," and "courteous and efficient service." Nothing negative was really said about the store, but enthusiasm for it was not evident either. Some people compared Schnuk's store with others in bigger cities and others in the surrounding area as well. Some even mentioned the new chain store in town, although they did not say anything really impressive about it. As was expected, most of the people interviewed were regular customers.

From this information, we see that the stores in Sebewaing and Gaylord have a steady clientele that enjoy shopping in the stores and are satisfied with the merchandise, prices, and service. The people shopping there are mostly from the immediate area and do the majority of their shopping at Schnuk Clothing stores. Another important statistic was noted: thirty-six of the sixty randomly selected for the survey were women.

Especially interesting to Mr. Schnuk was the results of question six of the survey. Only three out of sixty knew of and shopped at the store because of an advertisement. This pointed out that potentially new customers are not being reached by their advertising program.

At their next meeting, Mr. Schnuk and his two sons discussed the findings of the survey. In general, the results were as expected, except for their lag in advertising. Mr. Schnuk suggested that a larger percentage of their operating budget be redirected into advertising and special promotion campaigns. This would cut down on profits, but they all felt it was needed to keep up with the outstanding promotional program of their new competitor.

Question

> Evaluate Schnuk's promotion program in light of its new competition and the survey results.
>
> Devise a new promotion program.

THE VALLEY INN MOTEL
Declining Sales

The Valley Inn Motel is located on Park Street in downtown Flagstaff, Arizona, and consists of a 107-room motel, restaurant, and lounge bar. The motel itself has been doing exceptionally well, since it was purchased in 1973 by Humphrey Products Corporation. The Valley Inn was completely remodeled with modern furniture, color television, and a new swimming pool for its guests. The dining room (the Red Carpet Restaurant), located in the center of the complex, was also remodeled with new furniture and an elegant lounge.

The Restaurant's Problem

The major concern of the management at the moment lies with the restaurant. The excellent business and profit of the motel is not mirrored by the restaurant's success. Since Humphrey Products purchased the Valley Inn four years ago, the restaurant has not made a profit. By operating on the profit of the motel, it is kept open for the convenience of the motel guests.

Hours of operation

	Breakfast	7:00 AM – 11:30 AM
Monday thru Friday	Lunch	11:30 AM – 2:00 PM
	Dinner	5:00 PM – 9:00 PM
	Breakfast	8:00 AM – 11:30 AM
Saturday	Lunch	11:30 AM – 2:00 PM
	Dinner	5:00 PM – 9:00 PM
Sunday	Breakfast	8:00 AM – noon

Submitted by T. Jeff Goyert

The restaurant consists of three rooms which were set up to handle different-sized parties and the regular business. The rooms shown in Exhibit 9 can be rented for parties and a party menu with specialities is available.

The breakfast business during the week is below average. The customers consist of motel guests, businesspeople, and regulars. On Sunday, breakfast is the only meal served. The shift was set up to cater to the Sunday church crowd. The past two years, business has dropped remarkably, from an average of one hundred orders to thirty. The reason for the decline is not known. There have been no changes in employees or menu prices.

Exhibit 9   *Layout of Red Carpet restaurant*

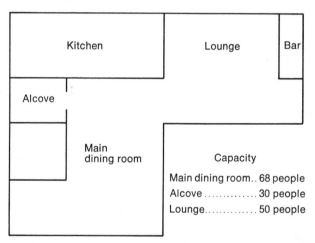

The weekly lunch hours are the busiest, mostly attracting local businesspeople on their lunch hours. The lunch hour requires the largest number of employees because of the speed at which orders

Exhibit 10   *Orders placed*

	Average number of orders	Number of orders to break even	Number of orders that can be served with present staff
Monday – Saturday			
Breakfast	57	65	150
Lunch	167	156	250
Dinner	29	58*	100*
Sunday			
Breakfast	34	75	200

*With a smorgasbord, 200 orders can be served and 62 are needed to break even.

must be served for customers to receive a quick lunch. With the high salary costs, there is a low margin of profit at these times. Saturday lunch draws the least amount of business; the only reason the restaurant is kept open is to serve the motel guests.

Dinner is the main concern. Business at this meal has never been profitable or made any improvement. The dinner hours mainly attract motel guests, couples, and some families.

Past Strategies

Many people have been questioned about the restaurant and comments have been made on the good food and service. There were no complaints on the prices; they were considered to be competitive. The most frequent comment made was that they never heard of the Red Carpet Restaurant. Many people explained they never knew the Valley Inn Motel had a dining room.

The management in 1975 tried offering at dinner an elaborate smorgasbord consisting of a twelve-bowl relish table and a meat bar with prime rib, ham, and turkey for $4.95 a plate — "all you can eat." The smorgasbord managed to draw more regular customers. The management never advertised the smorgasbord, since they believed in word of mouth advertising which went along with the advertising policy of the restaurant. The smorgasbord was in effect for seven weeks and then was dropped. There was not enough business to cover the extra labor cost of one cook that was used for slicing meat. Many employees and customers praised the smorgasbord and felt that all it needed was advertising to draw in customers. The discontinuation was a top-management decision.

Currently, the Red Carpet offers a "Happy Hour" in the lounge bar from 5 PM to 7 PM, Monday thru Friday, with the object being familiarizing people with the restaurant. All drinks are sold at $.50 during these hours. This feature is advertised only in the lobby of the motel. Having been in effect for nine weeks, it has drawn many people through the restaurant to the lounge, but there has been no substantial increase in food sales.

Exhibit 11   *Cost structure table (% of one dollar)*

	Food cost	Salary cost	Operating cost	Rent	Depreciation	Profit
What restaurant costs should be:	40%	25%	20%	6–9%	4%	2–5%
Red Carpet Restaurant:	43%	25%	17%	10%	6%	−1%

Red Carpet net income schedule

Year	Net income
1968	$18,935.00
1969	20,151.00 (remodeled)
1970	27,674.00
1971	36,288.00

Assessing The Problem

The salary costs are under control and acceptable by management. The employed crew on each shift is at a minimum but would be capable of serving more orders. The food costs are slightly higher than they should be. There is a study being conducted of the food costs by Gerry Paul, the head chef in the kitchen, in an attempt to lower the costs. Also, portion control, which decreases waste, is being adopted. The rent is a monthly mortgage of $6,000 for the motel and restaurant, and there is normal depreciation. There has been no profit since the restaurant was purchased; in fact, it has been running at a loss. Management is considering changing their present policies to find a solution to the problem.

What do people look for when eating out? A national survey taken in 1974 showed:

Cleanliness	67%
Good wholesome food	52
Service	46
Surroundings and atmosphere	42
How food is prepared	38
Price of food	33
Variety of food	19
Ways food is served	17
Quality of food	16
Types of food	13
Appearance of food	11
Is food hot?	9
Location of restaurant	9
Reputation of restaurant	9
Quantity of food	9

The following interview questions were asked of management by a marketing analyst.

1. What type of people would you like to attract to your restaurant?
We would like to attract businesspeople to our lunch hour and

breakfast. At the dinner shift, we feel the family is most important, along with couples who like to dine in a quiet relaxing atmosphere.

2. Your location is downtown Flagstaff on the north end. Does this have any effect on your business or the people you attract?
   At the lunch hour, the location is excellent, being close to many businesses. The location is a handicap for dinner, since many people are leary of going downtown at night because of the bad reputation of Flagstaff's downtown section.

3. Are the employees working efficiently?
   Our employees are very efficient. Most of them have been with the company for a long time.

4. Is the general employee relationship compatible or do you feel there should be employee changes?
   The employee relationship is very compatible; they work well together and with management. Everyone is working together to establish a profitable business.

5. Does the appearance of the food seem acceptable?
   Our orders are always garnished to provide an appetizing plate for the customers.

6. Is the food always hot when served?
   The food is prepared and immediately placed under heat lamps until served. All the orders are served within minutes of the preparation.

7. In your opinion, what type of reputation does the restaurant have among its customers?
   Many of the restaurant customers now are regulars and have said that the Red Carpet is a nice and relaxing place. The food is good and the service is very responsive.

8. Does the quality of food go along with the prices charged?
   There are no complaints on the quality of food, although it has been noticed that much of the food is not eaten.

9. Do you feel that the variety of food or the ways it is prepared have affected your business?
   Our food is prepared the same as most restaurants of the same quality. The menu is set up to provide a wide variety of meals. Our menu won a national award both for appearance and for variety.

10. Why did your attempt with the smorgasbord fail?
    The smorgasbord was a high-cost feature to run with its wide variety of food (the three meats offered and the twelve-bowl relish table). There was also the cost of having a cook to carve the meat.

11. Why, in your opinion, is the Happy Hour during the week not drawing any more customers?

The Happy Hour would attract more people except we have chosen not to advertise it so far. We may have to advertise in the near future.

12. The atmosphere in your dining room seems pleasant and relaxing. Does this coincide with what you want for attracting the type of customer desired?

    Yes, we feel that the people that we have mentioned before would enjoy dining in this type of atmosphere.

13. The dinner shift seems like it could possibly be eliminated. What are your feelings?

    We have considered this before, but the owner, Mr. Humphrey, has decided to keep it open. He is willing to incur the extra cost and try for a profitable shift.

14. Are there any suggestions you might have concerning the restaurant's operation or techniques which might be looked into to improve your turnover?

    The restaurant needs a gimmick to attract customers. An advertising campaign could be used to make it known. We would like to leave the situation open to you.

15. I understand there was almost no advertising on the smorgasbord that you ran. Do you think this was the cause of its failure?

    This is very possible; we decided not to advertise because we felt that it wasn't necessary.

16. Why was the management against advertising?

    We felt the cost was too great for what it was worth.

17. There is a small amount of advertising going on right now with your regular menu. Is it working?

    Our advertising has increased our business slightly but nothing overwhelming. The advertising is not extensive, only radio, with no prime time.

18. Has the Happy Hour you initiated been advertised other than in the lobby?

    No, we have kept it to the motel only.

19. What kind of advertising have you done in the past?

    Only radio advertising for the restaurant. We have billboard advertising for the motel in which we mention the restaurant.

20. Would you consider bringing back the smorgasbord?

    Yes, if it could be shown that it would be profitable.

21. Would a combination of the smorgasbord and the Happy Hour be feasible?

    Yes, we plan to keep the Happy Hour around for a while as it looks promising. If the smorgasbord would work, it could be very effective.

22. On your earlier smorgasbord you served prime rib, turkey, and ham. How would you feel about eliminating the ham and

turkey and keeping the elaborate relish tray (i.e. a limited smorgasbord)?

This might work; prime rib was the best seller anyway (90 percent of the people took prime rib).

23. Do you feel you should serve potatoes and vegetables on the smorgasbord?

Yes, this goes along with a full meal. They are inexpensive items.

Exhibit 12   *A sampling of the Red Carpet menu: the entrees portion*

The Red Carpet offers your favorite wines, champagnes, and professionally prepared cocktails.

Entrees

Special of the House	The Chef's Special
WESTERN STEAK	RIB-EYE STEAK
Served on Garlic Toast,	Served with Home-Style Toast,
Onion Rings, Hash Browns,	Tossed Salad, Dressing
Tossed Salad, Dressing	Onion Rings, Hash
and Beverage	Browns, Beverage
$5.25	$4.75

South African Lobster Tail
Broiled on the shell, served with drawn butter $7.75
Ship 'N' Shore
6-ounce filet, 6-ounce lobster tail, stuffed shrimp, onion ring $7.95
Boneless Rainbow Trout Maitre D'Hotel
12 to 14 ounces $4.95
Fried Jumbo Home Style Shrimp
Served with tangy sauce $5.50
Prime Filet Mignon
One-half pound, garnished chef-style $6.95
New York Cut Strip Sirloin Steak
Fully garnished, chef-style $6.95
Roast Sirloin of Beef Au Jus
Garnished, chef-style $3.95
U. S. Choice Chopped Sirloin
One-half pound, char-broiled with mushrooms $3.95
Golden Honey-Dipped Fried Chicken
Southern style $3.95
Center-Cut Pork Shops
Two 6-ounce chops served with apple sauce $4.25
Ham Steak with Pineapple Ring
One-half pound, garnished $3.95

All complete dinners include our relish tray, your choice of potatoes, vegetables, tossed salad, beverage, roll and butter.

Possible Alternatives

1. Set up an extensive advertising campaign with the present menu. Do a cost study on the food costs.
2. Revise the menu to include different gourmet dinners and advertise.
3. Perform a cost study on salaries, expenses, and food to determine where the profit is going. Raise menu prices, if necessary.
4. Set up a limited smorgasbord with the Happy Hour. Set up an extensive advertising campaign locally, including newspapers, prime-time radio, and possibly television.

Question

Systematically evaluate the Red Carpet operation and suggest a solution to its profit problem. Justify your suggestion.

ELECTRIC HEATERS FOR AUTOMOBILES
Evaluating a Marketing Program for a New Product

During the winter months, D. J. Fidd had developed and manufactured the electric heating units that he had been thinking of
putting on the market for quite some time. Only a few were manufactured for sample display and introduction.

Mr. Fidd had two models of a small electric heater which could
be used in an automobile to keep the inside temperature warm
enough that an ice and snow accumulation could not form on the
outside. By using the product, people would find a warm car in
the morning with no ice and snow to be scraped away. In addition,
the automobile's own defroster system would have less work to
do, and there would not be the required waiting period to clear
the frost from the inside of the windshield. One variation was the
portable model which could also be removed from the automobile
and used elsewhere. The second model has fewer components
than the portable model and would be adapted to the automobile's
heating system. Both models were 600-watt heaters.

Fidd's initial target market was the automobile owner without
a garage, and the heater would be promoted as an inexpensive
means of keeping the auto free of ice and snow. If the heater had
the expected acceptance by the user (as he believed it would),
Mr. Fidd intended offering heaters in larger wattage, particularly
a portable model for trucks, boats, campers, and trailers.

A possible use would be to keep moisture from damaging inte-
riors of stored boats or camping trailers during the winter months.
The safety feature of the unit would be two-fold. All units would
have an integral thermostat that would control the operation of

Submitted by Jerry Decker

the unit, since some variation in insulation of automobiles, for example, would have an effect upon the operation of the heating unit. In addition to the thermostat, there would be a thermal overload cutout, which would mean that the unit would not be able to overheat while it was left untended. Both models would have a cord running from the unit to the outside of the automobile's grill. This would then be attached to the power source of the homeowner.

Exhibit 13   *Product design*

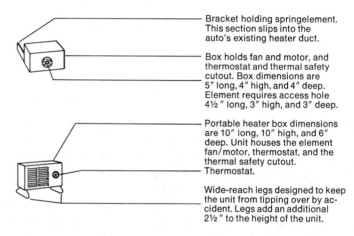

Bracket holding springelement. This section slips into the auto's existing heater duct.

Box holds fan and motor, and thermostat and thermal safety cutout. Box dimensions are 5" long, 4" high, and 4" deep. Element requires access hole 4½" long, 3" high, and 3" deep.

Portable heater box dimensions are 10" long, 10" high, and 6" deep. Unit houses the element fan/motor, thermostat, and the thermal safety cutout.
Thermostat.

Wide-reach legs designed to keep the unit from tipping over by accident. Legs add an additional 2½" to the height of the unit.

A component parts list and cost is shown in Exhibit 14. Cost of parts is shown for 500-lot quantities only. A substantial price decrease results if the parts are bought in the 1,000 or more quantity range. This decrease would amount to approximately 20 percent.

Integral unit prices for the introductory campaign would be $6.71 each at the wholesale level and $8.95 at the consumer level. The portable unit would cost $7.85 at the wholesale level and $10.95 at the consumer level. Mr. Fidd intended to publish his recommended list price in promotional campaigns and also to attempt to handle himself the distribution both at the wholesale and consumer levels. In both situations, the product would be shipped f.o.b. Mr. Fidd's production point, as the cost of packing and handling is not included in the cost of the products. He planned on using local delivery service exclusively during the introductory cycle of the product and on offering freight-free service to those outlets purchasing a combination of at least ten units.

Mr. Fidd's initial target market for the introductory campaign was to be New York City and the area within a seventy-mile radius. Introductory advertising would be conducted in the local news-

Exhibit 14   *Variable unit product cost*

Integral unit:	element	.80
	fan/motor	1.75
	safety cutout	1.00
	thermostat	1.00
	wire	.12
	cord cap	.03
		4.70 unit cost

Portable unit:	outershell	.80
	thermostat	1.00
	element	.80
	safety cutout	1.00
	fan motor	1.75
	cord cap	.03
	wire	.12
	legs	.04
		5.54 unit cost

papers covering the area, and specially designed brochures sent to the appliance, hardware, and automotive stores in the area. Local radio station coverage would also be used during the months of November through February of the introductory period. All advertising will particularly stress product benefits to the user, and the fact that any competitive product is too large in size and price to serve the same function. Additional promotional activity would include product display at the automobile and travel-trailer show.

Question

Evaluate the marketing program for this new product.

chapter

11

Societies, Governments, and Marketing Cases

CRATER PAPER COMPANY
Recycling Products

Introduction

Crater Paper Company is one of the leading manufacturers of quality text and cover papers in the United States. They are also one of the leading manufacturers of technical papers produced to the most exacting standards.

Crater has three mills: one in Vicksburg, Michigan; another in Ripon, California; and the third in Anderson, California. Their gross sales last year were approximately 70 million dollars. They are the thirty-sixth largest paper manufacturer in the United States, but one of the "big three" in the text and cover lines.

Most of the text and cover grades are classified as "fine" paper. The product is used in annual reports, folders, brochures, books, newsletters, house organs, envelopes, and most other end uses that would utilize a premium printing paper. If the printing job requires the best possible paper regardless of cost, Crater's paper will be used.

Marketing
100 Percent Recycled Paper

In November of 1971, the management of the Crater Paper Company was considering the possibility of launching a full-scale marketing drive for 100 percent recycled paper. Printing papers have been made for years with small dabs of recycled fiber, but no other company had considered a 100 percent recycled printing paper.

Submitted by Gary Huff, Marketing Manager, Classic Manufacturing Company

Crater, the year before, tried to market a 100 percent recycled book paper without success. "We didn't find much market acceptance," admits Frank Spatz, Crater's President. "If you showed the paper to five printers, you got six reasons why it wouldn't work." Above all, the printers said that 100 percent recycled paper was too porous and absorbent to get a clear printed image. Crater believes they have solved this problem by adding a chemical to the paper. Many potential customers are still not willing to take the risk and use 100 percent recycled paper.

Difficulties Involved in Manufacturing Recycled Paper
There have been problems. The major difficulties are the variable qualities and impurities of the raw material. "We get all kinds of extraneous material in our reclaimed paper." Spatz says. "In one bale of scrap, we even found a live cat." The most common contaminants encountered are paper clips and staples, wet-strength paper, rubber-bands, wood chips, and polyethylene.

There is a second class of contaminants that are extremely difficult to remove and cause problems far in excess of their percentage occurrence. Commonly called "pernicious contraries," the group includes such materials as self-adhesive tapes, heat-seal gums and pasting adhesives. A proportion of these pass through most screening systems, and because of their small size and their specific gravity of 0.9 – 1.0, they are not removed in centrifugal cleaners either. Problems arising from the above conditions include poor sheet transfer and holes in the sheets.

Advantages of Virgin Fibers
Unfortunately, many buyers prefer products made entirely or largely from virgin wood fibers. The growth of paper recycling has also suffered from increased labor and transportation costs. This has made it possible to make most grades of paper more efficiently and more profitably from new raw materials than they can be made from wastepaper fibers. Also, the papermaking equipment is more efficient in the plants using virgin wood fibers.

Waste Materials
The papermaking process generates large quantities of waste materials which must be disposed of in one way or another. Only about one-half of the weight of the original wood ends up as salable paper. The rest consists of bark, clay, wood sugars, starches, and other materials. While efforts have been made to convert some of these into other useful, salable materials, a large percentage must be disposed of by burning, land fill, or introduction into

nearby rivers or streams.[1] For the type of paper Crater produces, eighty-nine trees are equal to about 10,000 pounds of paper.

Raw Materials
Raw materials are purchased from dealers who collect scrap papers from industry, offices, printers, or converters. The dealers sort wastepaper into various grade levels. Crater buys only bleached paper, such as computer forms, tab cards, envelope clipping, and similar items. Much of the scrap is printed materials.

Exhibit 1   *Cost of waste paper*

There are five types of waste. Crater can only use the first two types because of the high quality of their paper.

1.	White printed paper	$325 – 335*
2.	White unprinted paper	335 – 340
3.	Mixtures of colored paper	55 – 65
4.	Unboiled paper	58 – 60
5.	Bad waste — such as mixtures paper and carbon paper	15 – 25

*Per ton

Price and Cost
De-inking and other reprocessing steps raise the cost per ton of recycled paper $20 to $40 above that made from virgin pulp. Crater's selling price to its wholesalers is comparable with its other text and cover brands that have been made from virgin pulp.

Tax
The virgin-pulp industry gets a depletion allowance for cutting timber and tax allowances for getting logs to the mill. The recycled-paper manufacturer gets no such allowances.

Marketing Policies and Practices for 100 Percent Recycled Paper

The social responsibility and ecology theme is the marketing justification for selling 100 percent recycled paper. The customer must be persuaded that recycled paper is worth the added cost, since the recycling saves trees and recovers part of the waste now inundating cities.

Crater had developed a "watermark" which identifies each sheet as being 100 percent recycled paper. Customers are proud

---

1. J. H. Jordan, Jr., "Making Money With Waste Paper," *Graphic Arts Monthly*, Vol. 43 (April, 1971), p. 49.

to have this symbol on their paper, since its significance is then communicated to their consuming public.

Crater is prepared to make an extensive promotional campaign for 100 percent recycled paper.

Final
Comment

Crater's past efforts with recycled paper have drawn cheers from conservationists. The Sierra Club wrote Crater a letter of commendation, and the club is hiring a representative to persuade companies to use recycled paper and to urge more papermakers to produce it.

Crater's management is known throughout the industry as being very progressive and very concerned with ecology. The Vicksburg mill is the leading mill in the country in controlling water and air pollution.

At least one papermaker regards 100 percent recycled paper as a passing fad brought on by misplaced environmental concern. "It's purely a gimmick for a few companies," declares the president of one of Crater's competitors.

Crater's management feels it is possible to manufacture high-quality printing papers from 100 percent waste paper. The management of Crater feels they can eventually contribute to their total profit picture by introducing a recycled line of paper to supplement their other lines. Also, the people of Crater have a sincere interest and pride in contributing to the improvement of the environment. But, to be successful, it will require increased consumer acceptance or demand for recycled paper products and development of new products that utilize reclaimed fibers. At the paper mill level, it requires improvement in the economics of recycling, along with local and federal legislation. Currently, 11.5 million tons of paper are being recycled. About 70 percent goes into boxboard and container boards, fiber products, recycled newsprint, and building products. A very small percentage of recycled fiber goes into printing paper.

The recycled paper will be used to supplement Crater's other text and cover lines. It can be used in annual reports, folders, brochures, and most other end uses that would utilize a premium printing paper. Visual and physical characteristics of Crater 100 percent recycled paper are quite similar to a nonrecycled grade in a comparable price range. Recycled papers are subject to more variations in shades of white and also in two-sideness of colors than paper made from virgin fibers. There are also a greater number of visible spots within the paper.

At present Crater advertises its products in trade journals, in brochures sent to wholesalers, and in regional additions of *Business Week.*

Questions

What strategy should Crater use to gain acceptance of recycled paper?

What are other ways Crater might show that it is a socially responsible company?

What benefits and risks is Crater incurring in trying to market recycled paper?

V & V APPLIANCES
Store Location

V & V Appliances was the oldest appliance outlet in a midwestern city of 200,000. The company had been in business for nearly twenty-five years. The company had started out as a hardware and paint store but soon became a primary outlet for appliances. The original store was located in what was the richest section of town twenty-five years ago. Now, this area has become the heart of the low-rent district of the city. Ten years ago, one of the original owners, Mr. Van, bought out his partner, Viss, who needed the money. Mr. Van continued quite successfully for the next five years. Then competition became very stiff. Many new discount stores opened up with large appliance departments. Along with these, many new chain appliance stores opened in the city. Both of these types of outlets were advertising considerably, making it difficult for V & V to get new customers.

Mr. Van decided he should look for a new partner and try to open another store in a better area. This, he felt, was a good decision because he could afford more advertising with the added capital, and it would also be a selling point to have two locations to serve customers. He found his partner and in 1970 opened a store in a growing area in the south end of town.

Since the new store opened, sales have depended heavily on the outside new-home building business brought in by their one traveling salesperson. The old store continually had trouble keeping sales from dropping and this store was also robbed six times in a period of two years, which was causing the insurance company to threaten to cut off V & V's benefits.

Submitted by Fred Postema

With the increased tight-money situation, many people had quit buying such items as televisions, dishwashers, and stereo sets. Also, the new-home building industry had nearly dropped to nothing in two years. These two factors contributed heavily to the difficult situation in which V & V now found itself.

V & V Appliances were known by the public to be honest and reliable businesspeople. With this as one of the company's main policy objectives, V & V often found themselves giving much more service to their customers than did most of the other appliance outlets. Mr. Van felt that even though this service was costly, it was one of the important reasons why V & V had kept many of its customers for twenty-five years.

V & V sold many name brand appliances as follows:

TV and stereo	*White goods*
Zenith	Hotpoint
Motorola	Tappan
Packard Bell	Gibson
	Roper
Small appliances	Caloric
Eureka	Hardwick
Sunbeam	Kelvinator
Hoover	Enterprise

The profit margin on most white-goods appliances was 25 percent of cost. Televisions and stereos had a slim profit margin of approximately 15 percent of cost. Small appliances had so little profit that they were kept solely for the convenience of the customer.

Some basic facts above V & V sales are:
Gross sales for the old store amount to $90,000 per year.
Gross sales for new store amount to $150,000 per year.
A. Inventory turnover:
   White goods — five times per year
   Small appliances — two times per year
   Television and stereos — two times per year
B. Average inventory investments equal $50,000.
C. Average cost per delivery of one item comes to $10.00.
D. Total cost of advertising in 1975 was $1000.

Inventory — January, 1975
   13 stereos
   20 black-and-white portables
   10 color consoles
    6 color portables

40 gas ranges
25 electric ranges
20 washers
17 dryers
20 dishwashers
50 small appliances
35 refrigerators

Question

Should V & V continue its store in the low-rent district? Justify your answer.

FOODS, INC.
Advertising a Firm's Concern and Efforts to Improve the Environment

The board of directors of Foods, Inc., in considering the planned advertising campaign for the current year, are in disagreement over the national television promotion. The budget has been agreed upon; however, how best to use the nationwide coverage is under consideration.

The disagreement centers on whether or not time should be allotted to advertising the antipollution campaign Foods, Inc., has implemented. Some members feel it should be included because of the goodwill that would be generated. These members feel it would definitely benefit the company to advertise the lead Foods has taken toward stopping the pollution associated with the processing of Foods products. Other members feel that, although it would not be a complete waste of money, it is not necessary. If time is allotted to advertising the antipollution campaign, these members feel not enough time could be spent on promoting Foods products, especially any new products being introduced or those that may be introduced in the near future.

Because the new television campaign is centered on a current theme, the disagreement must be solved soon. Failure to solve it could result in the advertisements being implemented too late, possibly resulting in a decline in effectiveness.

The Company

Foods, Inc., was founded in 1869. Since that time, it has grown to include seven plants. It is primarily a grape-processing company.

Submitted by Ronald E. Haywood, Service Merchandiser, Spartan Stores, Inc.

However, the variety of products has grown to include other fruit products as well. Foods Inc., as the processing and marketing subsidiary of The Grape Association, Inc., distributes some forty varieties of juices, jellies, and preserves to over 200,000 food stores in the United States and fifty-one foreign countries, as well as the food service industry. Exhibit 2 shows the record of net sales over a ten-year period.

Exhibit 2   *Ten-year summary of net sales*

1966	$49,485,232
1967	55,434,625
1968	58,426,959
1969	58,842,745
1970	59,532,034
1971	59,120,368
1972	65,107,672
1973	68,117,040
1974	70,591,684
1975	88,732,686

Pollution

Foods is a food-processing and marketing company. But before that, it is a land-use company. It lives from the land. Since 1869, Foods has always depended on the harvest for its livelihood. Today, more than 32,000 acres of vineyards contribute to its success. Because Foods depends so much on the land, it has always taken the position of not purposely abusing it, but instead trying to insure that future generations will be able to profit from it. Each of the seven plants has taken steps in a combined effort to prevent pollution.

Foods, Inc., has been a leader in fighting three types of pollution: air, water, and solid wastes. Although not all the problems have been solved, Foods is constantly investigating current methods and looking for more effective methods. Management knows full well the potential pollution that processing plants can cause for the communities in which they function. And since food is processed for people, it is in the best interests of the company's customers that the company help to make the environment as clean and wholesome as possible. The company motto is: We will not spoil the air, water, or land.

The steps Foods, Inc., has taken to stop pollution are presently advertised in pamphlets only. These booklets are distributed to interested parties without cost. No national advertising has been used to make the public aware of the leadership role Foods has assumed in pollution abatement. Because of the consumer movement to clean up the environment, business has borne the force of the attack of not doing enough. According to David Rockefeller, business must respond to these criticisms through consistently better performance effectively communicated.

However, Foods also has a responsibility to make a profit. Without an adequate profit, the fight against pollution could not be continued. If products are not advertised, they are not sold. A nationwide television advertising campaign is an expensive undertaking. How it can be used most effectively is definitely a difficult decision.

Questions

What should the advertising strategy be?

Can both products and pollution efforts be effectively promoted in a single advertisement?

THE SOUTH MOST LIFE INSURANCE COMPANY
Stimulating the Need for Insurance

J. W. Schlitz is the President of South Most Life Insurance Company. J. W. owns 66 percent of South Most. He originally started the firm in 1947 after serving in the military until 1945 and spending the next two years as a very successful life insurance salesman with a national firm. J. W. slowly built South Most through the years into a reputable insurance company. Assets and sales make South Most the seventy-eighth largest life insurance company in the United States. Like most life insurance companies, South Most is constantly working to increase the amount of life insurance in force and, like most, it sells largely through the efforts of a sales force. Recruiting, training, and maintaining the sales force is a constant challenge. New salespeople have a high turnover rate; few last the first year.

A possible solution to increasing insurance in force and decreasing the problems with the sales force is virus, diluted type "X." Virus, diluted type "X," was developed by Karl Schlitz, chemist son of J. W. Schlitz. Type "X" produces symptoms similar to those of a mild heart attack: shortness of breath, chest pains, and the like. Once introduced into the body, the virus diluted type "X" symptoms will last approximately two months, with the most intense symptoms occurring within twenty-four hours after diluted type "X" is introduced into the body. The effects diminish over the two-month period.

Although the symptoms are similar to mild heart attacks, the effects are in the nervous system, not actually in the heart. Be-

---

This is an imaginary case, but it is certainly not outside the realm of possibility.

cause the symptoms are in the nervous system and not in the heart, a physician would not mistakenly diagnose type "X" as a heart attack. In fact, a physician would probably conclude the individual had some psychosomatic problems that would go away with time. Thus, the individual would probably be given a "clean bill of health" report by a physician if the individual's only problem was infection with diluted type "X."

Originally, virus type "X" was developed by defense department chemists for germ warfare. As originally developed, full-strength type "X" virus affected males from fifteen to forty years of age and caused incapacitating chest pains for a forty-eight-hour period, with the individual completely recovering after six months. Karl Schlitz had been a chemist for the defense department and had illegally taken a sample of type "X" virus from the defense department's research laboratory. His only reason for taking the sample had been his complete fascination as a chemist with the virus. The virus's selectivity for males of a certain age range and its nervous system affliction was puzzling to Karl.

Karl had resigned his commission and had for the last two years been working as a chemist for Oceanflow Petroleum Company. He no longer worked with viruses as a part of his job, but his interest in type "X" had remained. As a hobby he has continued to work with type "X" in his basement laboratory. He had set out to develop an antidote for the virus. After considerable work, his only accomplishment had been to develop a diluted strain of the virus. The ability to dilute the virus was an exciting step in the right direction, but an antidote was a long way from being developed.

Diluted type "X" affects men in the range from twenty-five to fifty-five years of age. It also survives in adverse environments from seven to ten days. It is not contagious. Direct inhalation of air heavily laden with the virus was the easiest way for an individual to become affected. But, since the virus did not settle in the respiratory system, it was extremely difficult for an individual to infect another — even kissing was not likely to pass the virus.

J. W. had discovered his son's work with diluted type "X" and immediately envisioned an application. Being in the life insurance business, J. W. knew that many people thought only about life insurance when they were not feeling their best and would willingly buy life insurance then. Quite frequently they could not qualify at this point. An exposure to a heavy dose of diluted type "X" and to South Most Life Insurance literature would sell a lot of life insurance. J. W. had the idea of sending the two together in one envelope to prospects (Exhibit 3).

Exhibit 3   *Card to be sent to prospect*

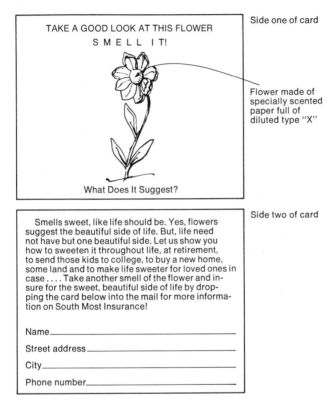

Side one of card

TAKE A GOOD LOOK AT THIS FLOWER
S M E L L   I T!

Flower made of
specially scented
paper full of
diluted type "X"

What Does It Suggest?

Side two of card

Smells sweet, like life should be. Yes, flowers
suggest the beautiful side of life. But, life need
not have but one beautiful side. Let us show you
how to sweeten it throughout life, at retirement,
to send those kids to college, to buy a new home,
some land and to make life sweeter for loved ones in
case . . . . Take another smell of the flower and insure for the sweet, beautiful side of life by dropping the card below into the mail for more information on South Most Insurance!

Name————————————————————
Street address—————————————————
City——————————————————————
Phone number————————————————

J. W. initially wants to send these cards out to wealthier men
of the region. They are more likely prospects for larger policies.
If it seems to work effectively, other potential policy purchasers
could be sent this card. J. W. has tried for the last year to sell a
$250,000 policy to D. W. Lorsely, a wealthy businessman. Re-
cently, J. W. sent Mr. Lorsely a sample card he made up. In this
morning's mail, Jim received a letter from D. W. Lorsely suggest-
ing he was in the market to buy a $1,500,000 policy and would like
to talk to J. W.

Question

*Should this technique be tried by the South Most Company? In
justifying your answer, be sure to include a discussion of the
ethical issues involved in this decision.*

12

Marketing Ideas, Concepts and Solutions

A & B DISPLAY

A & B Display is a small manufacturing firm in Sandusky, Ohio. The company's product is display racks for cookies and cakes. Ownership in the partnership is shared by Wendell Allen and Phil Bowers. Allen is the son-in-law of Bowers. Bowers' other daughter works as a secretary, and does not get along with Mr. Allen. Allen and Bowers are both certified pattern makers, and Allen works in Bowers' pattern shop.

The two partners have shown opposite attitudes towards expansion. Bowers is sixty-two years old, very wealthy and wishes to sit on his money. Allen is thirty-five and feels that A & B Display has considerable potential for growth. A & B sells almost all of its present production to Freshly cookies. Bowers would like to get a tying contract with Freshly, where each would be committed to the other. Freshly has shown no interest in a tying agreement, but they do not want A & B to sell to any of Freshly's direct competitors. A & B has honored this desire, because Freshly is providing almost the entire sales volume. Recently, however, Nancy's Cookies has shown considerable interest in A & B display racks.

The racks which A & B produces are semipermanent. They are easily assembled and disassembled, and are not intended to be permanent store fixtures. They are wooden with chrome trim around the edges of the shelves, in various sizes and three colors: white, pink, and green. The rack is then veiled with a fine black spray, which gives it a mottled effect. The sizes range in width from twenty-four inches to forty-eight inches; all are six feet in height.

Submitted by Patrick M. McCann, Manager, Marshalltron and Metal Company, Battle Creek

Prices run from $24 for the twenty-four inch rack to $32 for the forty-eight inch rack.

The racks were designed by Bowers in 1955. He applied for the patent then, and received it in February, 1962. The patent covers thirteen points on the rack, mostly its ability to break down for easy shipment and storage.

The racks were first made in the pattern shop by Edward Nudding, who was hired full-time especially for this purpose. When he would get behind, Allen would help him until production caught up with orders. In the early years, the racks were sold to anyone who ordered them. In 1960, however, Freshly Cookies began a program of standardizing its national advertising, and they believed that the A & B display rack fit the company image. They decided to buy all their display racks from A & B. The individual companies in Freshly were told to buy A & B racks or find identical substitutes. Because Freshly has its national office in Sandusky, it was easy to negotiate an agreement. A & B was glad for this opportunity to expand sales and profits.

Freshly is a nationwide system of independent bakeries. They have bakeries located in twenty-two different states, with a national office in Sandusky, Ohio. They bake and sell mostly hard cookies under the slogan, 'Home Style Cookies.'' The company is highly decentralized with each bakery responsible for profits. The national office controls only overall company policy. Thus, each bakery bought its display rack needs directly from A & B, which would then install the racks in the store free of cost to the store. The price of the racks was not important, as long as they fit the company image.

Freshly said they would require $70,000 a year in display racks. With this in mind, Allen wanted to build a new building and buy new equipment. At first Bowers balked at the expenditure, but Allen was able to convince him of the value of the project. The building was built in the early 1970s at a cost of $100,000 and four new employees were added. Later, it was found necesary to hire part-time help in the summer.

Cookie sales are generally much greater in winter months than in the summer months. However, there was an inverse relationship between the season when most cookies are bought and the time when racks are bought. A high concentration of rack sales in the summer was the result of low sales, reflecting the producers' attempts at using gimmicks and displays to bolster sales. Four-fifths of A & B orders were received from April to August. This caused problems for Allen and Bowers. Because they had a very close personal relationship with their employees, they would not lay them off. Instead, in the off-season they gave them menial work to do that would not contribute to profits. They tried to predict sales so that they could warehouse racks during the slack periods, but they were never successful at this endeavor and always ended up rushing in the summer.

In 1976, Nancy's Cookies, another cookie producer, sent a representative to A & B and expressed a desire to buy the display rack for Nancy's line. They said they felt they could guarantee A & B over $100,000 in business per year. A & B felt they could handle this production and still produce the Freshly racks, which had reached a sales of $140,000 annually. They might have to add an additional employee or increase their summer help.

Nancy's is owned by McKee enterprises of Collegedale, Tennessee. The entire organization is controlled and run by the Seventh Day Adventist Church. Nancy's main products are soft cookies and cakes. They would buy the racks without restrictions upon A & B.

Nancy's Cookies is a national organization with sales in all forty-eight contiguous states. All cookies are baked in Collegedale and distributed to nonfranchised stores. All racks would be ordered from Collegedale and distributed on this basis also. The price of the rack would be included in the price of the cookies; the store would be given a rack with an order of so many cartons of cookies. The system was highly centralized, with all decisions coming from Collegedale.

Allen feels that selling to Nancy's is a great opportunity for A & B Display to expand sales. He feels that besides the advantage of increasing sales, A & B would be less at the mercy of Freshly and would gain an independence never before possible. He also thinks that this would be a way to halt seasonal slacks in production. Bowers, on the other hand, is skeptical. He does not want to alienate Freshly, which has proven to be a steady and growing customer. He is afraid that Freshly would consider Nancy's a direct competitor and stop buying the A & B racks.

In further talks between Allen and Bowers, a number of additional points were discussed:

1. Freshly would probably argue that any company producing baked goods is in direct competition with them. Moreover, Nancy's distributes nationally. However, Freshly produces hard cookies, while Nancy's is limited to soft cookies and cakes.
2. Because Freshly's national office is located in Sandusky, A & B should be able to meet face to face with them on the proposal.
3. Nancy's might be willing to reveal what stores they sell in. Possibly there would be little conflict, because Freshly uses

a franchise operation. Where there is a conflict, Nancy's might be willing to accept a suitable substitute.

4. Bowers is reactionary to a degree, but can be persuaded to expand if profits are high. He proved this when he agreed to invest in the new building.

5. Other cookie companies have shown an interest in the A & B racks as evidenced by $14,000 in miscellaneous sales.

6. Selling to Nancy's would require year-round production.

7. Profits from Nancy's would warrant the risk of a Freshly pull-out. If Freshly considered Nancy's a competitor, there is reason to believe they would make a similar assessment of most of the other companies who would be interested in the rack. This would greatly reduce A & B's chances of ever expanding. Nancy's would place no such restrictions on A & B's sales.

8. Slack periods can be avoided by increased sales, expansion into other fields, or by getting better-spaced orders.

9. A & B feels capable of producing all of Nancy's needs, along with Freshly's, under the current system. Hiring additional summer help would easily accomplish this. If part-time help proved inadequate an additional full-time employee could be hired. Production could also go to two shifts with the available workforce.

10. It would be difficult for Freshly to spread out the orders because of their decentralized structure (in contrast to Nancy's system).

11. Expansion of sales seems a certainty for A & B display.

12. There seems to be an excellent market for A & B's racks.

Questions

What should A & B management do? If you suggest selling to Nancy's, assume the position of Mr. Allen and devise a strategy to win acceptance of Bowers and Freshly (don't lose their business).

If you suggest restricting sales to Freshly, assume the position of Bowers and devise a strategy to win acceptance from Allen and remain in the good grace of Nancy's for possible future sales.

SANFORD GRAIN COMPANY
Which Markets To Focus On

The Sanford Grain Company was founded in 1919. It was started by Jim Sanford and has been in the family ever since. The company started out as one grain elevator, and has grown to fifteen elevators state-wide. The company has been receiving average industry returns, 18 to 20 percent on their investment; but, in the last three years, profits and sales have been declining substantially.

Sanford's competition comes from three sources: Canada International, Purina Food Corporation, and DeKalb Grain Products. All these companies produce dog food and are in the grain business competing with Sanford.

Sanford Grain Company buys and sells grain and food supplement products for animals. In 1964, they started to produce and sell dog food. The dog food was sold under the label of Wayne dog food. The Sanford management believed that the dog food business would help sales during the off months of the year and during winter when business was the slowest.

With the declining population on small farms and the increase of larger farms buying their own grinding equipment, Sanford has changed ideas on grinding and animal food supplements. The trend now is to order only certain products. If a farmer wants a product not on hand, it will be ordered for him. Previously elevators used to keep on hand all the products available, but the lack of demand for certain products stimulated a change to the present system. With this philosophy, some of the Sanford elevators turned their interest and investments to the dog food business.

Submitted by Lawrence Delekta, Sales Manager, Allenton, Michigan

Sanford Company acts as a wholesaler and sells directly to the retailer. They have fifteen salespeople, one to represent each of the elevators. Each salesperson represents a district and reports back to the main office at Sanford. In the dog food business, the salesperson does not have to do any personal selling. In fact, the retailer calls the closest outlet for delivery of the product. The salesperson just makes sure that the buyer gets the order on time. This is a quite different procedure from selling grain and other products. When selling these products, the sales personnel call on the large retail outlets; otherwise, they have no contact at all with the customers that buy their products at the elevator. The elevator company also works as a retailer when it comes to the animal food supplements and some of the grains. However, dog food is always sold to retailers and is not pushed at the elevator.

Each one of the fifteen elevators owns its own trucks, and supplies the retailers in their area. They also sometimes carry on their own promotions.

The advertising is done by the main office. Advertising is placed in all the farm magazines, and starting soon, there will be advertising in a few dog and animal publications. Sanford has no extensive promotional programs for the grain business, but has been developing some for the dog food business. This advertising is done in magazines, posters, and educational pamphlets.

The market for grain has been decreasing. Since 1967, when the government put the subsidy program in, the market has steadily been dropping along with prices. On the other hand, the dog food market has been increasing. During the last board meeting, the suggestion was made to drop all promotions and advertising on grain and animal food supplements and concentrate exclusively on dog food.

Mr. Smith, one of the board members, commented on how sales were falling off with the grain products and that advertising would not bring up the sales substantially.

Mr. Thompson, on the other hand, said that the advertising was simply not hitting the target market any longer, and that farmers were not reading *Farm Journal, Successful Farmer,* and *Farm Management.* These magazines were read by the larger farmers and not by the farmers that were buying the Sanford products. He suggested that more advertising be directed toward the small farmer instead of the large farms which grind their own feed.

Mr. Maynard, head of promotions and advertising, said that individual elevator managers would not cooperate with him on promotions. He said that the elevator managers believe that the grain business is going out and that their main concern should be the dog food business. Mr. Maynard also believed that, with a new direction in advertising and a new approach in promotion, the grain market would be on the rise again.

Some of the ideas Mr. Maynard suggested were that Sanford send out more pamphlets on its products to all the farmers in the area, that advertising in *Farm Journal* and *Successful Farmer* be continued, but *Farm Management* be dropped. He believes that *Farm Management* is too sophisticated for the small farmer and is oriented toward the larger farmer. He also believes that advertising on radio stations that give farm reports in each area be conducted. This he believes will reach the farmer because more farmers are getting radios on tractors and they listen to the radio more now than before.

After Mr. Maynard gave his viewpoint, Mr. Shock, the manager of the Yale elevator, said that he was talking with one of his competitors and he had shown him that their sales on grain had been going up substantially, but would not give any reason why. Mr. Shock blames the advertising department for not doing its job, and he also claims that they never give him enough advance notice of the promotions that are planned.

Mr. Peterson, a head of sales department, denied the charge that it was the sales force's fault for not putting more effort into selling the grain products where commissions are not as high as in the dog food business. He blames the advertising department for not educating the retailer and customers and familiarizing them with the product. Mr. Peterson also pointed out that sales in the

Exhibit 1   *Dog food market*

Company	1972 Sales of grain and food (in tons)	Share of market
Sanford	1,200,806 tons	10.0%
Capac	1,000,005 tons	8.5%
Canada International	1,409,900 tons	24.1%
Purina Food Coop	1,420,000 tons	26.2%
DeKalb Grain Products	1,415,000 tons	25.4%
Independent	715,000 tons	5.8%
TOTAL	7,196,711 tons	100.0%

grain market are only 10 percent of the total company sales. Sales in tons have been dropping substantially. He said that there is not much grain grown in the area any more. Some of the reasons are: prices on grain crops, farmers are turning away and going into the dairy business or growing vegetables — some are even giving up farming completely.

Exhibit 2   *Company grain sales*

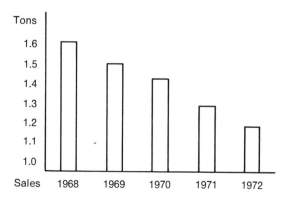

Each of the fifteen elevator managers gave a report and summed up what she or he thought was the major reason for the drop in the grain business and made suggestions of future strategy. The board members had differing opinions on these theories.
The meeting was adjourned until the following week.

Exhibit 3   *Advertising costs*

Publication	Space	Cost
Farm Journal	Full page monthly	$ 2,840,00
Successful Farmer	Full page monthly	$ 2,175,40
Farm Management	Full page monthly	$ 2,001,20
Progressive Farmer	Full page monthly	$ 1,500,80
Forecast	Full page monthly	$ 800.00
Grain Supplement	Two full pages weekly	$ 1,100.00
Total cost		$10,497.30

Question

What should Sanford emphasize? How? Assume the position of an individual advocating the area of emphasis you recommend and develop a strategy to win acceptance from other board members who may be advocating other areas.

SNACK BARS
Improving Operations of a Non-profit Business

There are three snack bars located on the campus of State University. There is the main snack bar located on Main Campus in the student center. It has a seating capacity of approximately 900 people. Also, there is a snack bar on East Campus in Wood Union. The third snack bar is located in the second dormitory complex in Gold Valley. The last two snack bars are smaller operations than the main union and have approximately half the seating capacity.

All three snack bars are under the supervision of one person. She makes most of the major policy decisions and must answer for them to higher officials for the university. Her actions must be justifiable and are subject to review on demand by her superiors.

The objectives of the snack bars are in some ways contradictory. The main objective of the department is service. The aim is to give the student what she/he wants if it is at all possible. Meeting student desires means high quality, variety, fast service, low prices, and many special services not ordinarily in line with food industry practices. These special services include such things as free disposable tableware to those who bring their own food, a large area for gathering due to slow turnover at the tables, setting up stage areas for special events which means extra cleaning, and other things in general which all add to the overhead.

It is difficult enough to find the proper mix to provide quality food and low prices, but the second objective of the snack bars is to make a profit. The first objective of making the students happy has been filled very well. A recent survey has shown that students are basically satisfied with the food and service and are not inter-

Submitted by Michael Dunphey

ested in higher prices for any reason. This poses a problem for the manager because profit is not possible without raising prices. Collectively, the snack bars have never shown a profit or broken even.

Now that the legislature is cutting back drastically on subsidies to the university, it is becoming imperative that the snack bars start showing a profit. What has brought this to the director's attention is an offer by an independent catering service to take over the entire operation. They propose to eliminate present food operations and replace them with vending machines offering a wide variety of beverages and foods. In addition, they guarantee the director a fixed profit which, combined with the annual loss, will mean a net gain of approximately $35,000 over the present results.

This seems very attractive, but will it satisfy the first objective of keeping the students happy? Possibly there could be something wrong with the hours of operation. She could close down during slower hours when not as many people use the facilities. The hours have previously been the result of considering the class hours in nearby buildings, relaxation hours, dinner hours, and union requirements that the full-time employees get a forty-hour week.

Since the director is faced with keeping the customers happy, she feels they should try to find other ways of reducing costs.

Another possibility is to cut the number of employees working for the snack bars. The problems that must be answered here are: Can the number of employees be reduced without decreasing the fast service desired? Will the union allow her to reduce the number of employees? Would this reduction show up as a sizeable amount of savings? The director is not sure how many people are needed, because the union will not allow her to lay off workers for an experiment. The union also makes it very difficult to fire an employee.

A variation of the above possibility might be to reduce wages. This, however, seems unlikely, since the union is constantly asking for higher wages and more benefits. It also should be noted that a sizeable portion of the work force is non-union employees who are students. They work for $.50 an hour less than union employees and are used on a part-time basis. The director does not know if these students could replace some of the full-time employees at various jobs.

The work schedules tend to be patterned after traffic flow through the register. This is a fairly predictable basis of scheduling, since class schedules follow the same pattern every week. There are also semester changes in the traffic flow of customers which are taken into account. It has also been found that there are quite a few repeat customers. The staff can recognize most of the customers after a few weeks into a new semester. It is further proposed that many customers account for numerous purchases on the same day. This would indicate that there are prospective customers who for some reason are not using the facilities. The director might increase profit if she can find some way to draw in these people.

Purchasing of supplies is done with respect to available storage facilities and freshness consideration. Effort has been made to take advantage of bulk discounts, where available, and competitive purchasing is judged with respect to value.

There are only certain times of the day when the snack bars reach full capacity. In the main union and Wood, it is at the noon hour. The Valley has its biggest rush around eight at night. These factors do not hold any sizeable significance. The unions each have their own appeal and do not infringe upon one another.

Apparently the customers are sincere in their desire for service as defined. Attempts in other directions have met with little success. Management's concern right now is profit. The automated alternative looks appealing; the only drawback is the refusal of the caterer to provide the special services desired by the students.

SUMMARY

Hours of operation are influenced by union demands for forty-hour weeks. Profit is hampered by slow weekends at Wood and the main union. The union will not lay off any of its people and would not buy the automation threat. It is cheaper to use part-time help who are efficient. There are too many full-time workers who have security by seniority and do not give a full day's work for a full day's pay.

The customers are basically repeat business who are satisfied with present operation.

Question

> *Devise a plan for the supervisor. Show in detail how you would go about implementing it to win student, union, and administration acceptance.*

THE RESTAURANT
Making an Advertising Program
Acceptable to Management

In October of 1975, The Restaurant opened after undergoing extensive remodeling. Previously, the building had housed a noisy bar with a night club atmosphere. Mr. Peter Smith, a lawyer in Manhattan, Kansas, and Mr. James Johnson, an owner of several service stations in the area, who were partners in the night club, decided that after two years of losing money they would close down the night club and open a restaurant. They employed Mr. Don Klein to manage the new restaurant and be the chef. Mr. Klein had previously been the manager and chef at a private club in the area and had a reputation of being an outstanding cook. After about two months of remodeling, the restaurant opened.

Seven women and seven men — most of whom were college students — were hired as waiters and waitresses. Only two or three had had previous experience. Don and Jackie, the hostess and Don's wife, spent two weeks of intensive training each night with the new waitresses. The week of October, 1975, The Restaurant opened.

The basic philosophy of the new restaurant was to sell quality food at a low price, making volume the profit-motivating factor. Don started by having an eleven-item menu with prices ranging from $2.95 for pork chops to $4.95 for T-bone steak. Don's idea was that, by serving such good food at low prices, the people who came in would advertise The Restaurant by word of mouth to others. Don also advertised in the monthly Greater Manhattan Area Guidebook, a small magazine listing area restaurants and

Submitted by Henry R. Krueger, Jr., Sales Representative, Georgia-Pacific Corporation, Corpus Christi, Texas

bars. The magazine was distributed in area motels and hotels. The advertisement was small and cost $35 a month. The only other type of advertising was done by a sign on the front of the building that said a new restaurant was coming soon. After the October opening, the only other advertisement was the sign in front of the Restaurant showing there was a restaurant at the location.

Within about a month, business was flourishing, and volume was running about $30,000 a month. Food and bar costs, however, were very high—about 68 percent food costs and 45 percent bar costs. Normally, a 42 to 44 percent food cost and a 25 to 31 percent bar cost is preferable.

In March of 1976, Don Klein and Peter Smith, one of the partners, had a business disagreement and Don left The Restaurant. Mr. Smith then hired Mrs. Marge Van Dyke to manage the restaurant temporarily until a permanent manager could be found.

Business continued to be good through April, when the slow part of the year for the restaurant industry (May through September) came upon the restaurant. Up to this point, there was still no advertising except by word of mouth and in the Greater Manhattan Area Guidebook.

In May, 1976, a new manager was hired, Mr. Mike Allen. During the summer months, the restaurant saw three different chefs come and go. During these summer months, the advertising consisted of the Greater Manhattan Area Guidebook. Since Mike has taken over managing The Restaurant, his food and bar costs have reached the average where they should be. Food cost is presently running at 43 percent, and bar cost is about 31 percent. Prices have been raised slightly, but this was a necessity. When Don was manager, the profit margin was approximately $.01 on the dollar. Since Mike has taken over, the net profit margin has risen to $.05 on the dollar.

Mike also started advertising weekly in the Manhattan Gazette, as well as continuing to place advertisments in the Greater Manhattan Area Guidebook. His advertising cost per month is now about $120.

Sales have decreased since Don left the restaurant to an average of $22,000 to $25,000 a month. In October of 1976, Mr. George Jameson was hired as chef. He has had much experience in several fine restaurants in the Kansas City and Lawrence area. Since he took over cooking, the quality of the food has risen back to Don's original standard.

In a restaurant that does about $250,000 worth of gross sales, Mr. Allen must decide how much advertising is needed and what media should be used. He knows advertising should be aimed at The Restaurant's target market, the middle-class people. The restaurant is not seeking the youth market and does not have a child's plate on the menu.

Even though bar and food costs are in line, The Restaurant's food sales outnumber bar sales by a ratio of three to one. If the restaurant is to increase overall sales, this ratio should be reduced to a one and one-half or two to one, which is more desirable since more money is made at the bar. Mr. Allen must consider means to increase his liquor sales. Presently, there are twelve bar stools and two tables in the cocktail area at which people can sit and drink without eating.

Mr. Peter Smith, now sole owner, is not in favor of advertising. Mr. Allen must cope with this when deciding whether to advertise more. Like many smaller businesses, The Restaurant does not incorporate an advertising expense into its yearly budget.

Question

Devise an advertising program which Mr. Peter Smith will accept. Justify your answer.

Appendix

Presenting Your Case

Do not be misled into thinking that because your logic in analyzing a problem adds up, your decision or program will automatically be accepted and implemented. Assuming that your logic really does add up, the task of winning support should be much easier — *you* should believe in the solution, at least. Never overlook the emotional, however, in working for support; it plays a significant role in persuasion.

You have to *sell* people on the *merits* of your decision to *win* support. This statement is true more often than may be realized. It is true if you are presenting a case from a marketing management, case-oriented textbook, needing the support of fellow students and your instructor; it is true if you are the vice president of marketing presenting a program to fellow executives and the chairman of the board; it is true if you are the autocratic owner of a company presenting *"the* decision" to your employees. People have a choice: at the very minimum they can accept or reject. Even though you have it in your power to make rejection costly to the person who selects that route, it is still a possible choice.

The more you sell, the larger your commitment to fulfill your promises. Few people will accept or give support on future occasions if the program or decision fails to deliver to them. But greater delivery than expected on consecutive occasions will lead to more easily obtainable support. Therefore, take time to analyze how much you believe in the correctness of the decision.

An analysis helps in another way. The more you believe in the decision, the more enthused you will be; the more enthused you are, the more it will show and the easier you will be able to sell.

Basic Elements of Presenting a Case

There are four elements common to all presentations — both written and oral.* A well-founded knowledge of each improves the chances of support. An audience, the presentation (program or decision), the speaker, and the situation make up the major elements of a presentation. The element's relationships are shown in Exhibit 1.

Exhibit 1   *Elements of a case presentation*

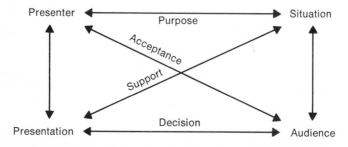

The outcome desired from the interaction of these elements is support for the program presented. With sufficient authority, an occasional program or decision can be pushed through without support — as in the case of an unpopular decision — but this is limited by the support for the authority. The ideal would be support from every individual affected; however, this response is both unlikely and unnecessary. Even with unpopular decisions, an effort should be made to explain why a decision is necessary before it is implemented.

In summary, the key to successful presentation is: know your audience, know your decision or program, know yourself, and know the situation.

Your Audience

You may have little to say about who is in the audience — a typical situation. On some occasions, however, the audience can be partially determined by you. If the audience is selected, the task of obtaining

---

*Although the discussion that follows is in terms of oral presentations, most of the suggestions made pertain to written presentations as well.

support is slightly easier. The audience can be divided into smaller homogeneous groupings instead of one large audience. Dividing allows patterning of the presentation to make it more convincing to each group — a divide and conquer strategy.[1] Dividing also allows greater freedom to answer individual questions.

Let's assume, however, that the audience is self-selecting or selected by someone else, and work with winning support in this more difficult environment. Even though the audience is self-selecting or selected by someone else, it is possible to accumulate information about that audience beforehand.[2] Information on general interests, age, education, occupation, problems, and the like, can be obtained with respect to the audience as a whole, even though the characteristics of individuals are unavailable. The famous comedian Bob Hope has entertained groups into the thousands of people with jokes about events peculiar to the group being entertained. Both he and his writers take the time to find out as much about the audience as a group as possible, even though they have little, if any, information about particular individuals in the audience.

Many an after-dinner speaker uses the dinner as a time to find out even more about the group from people at the head table. Within a small organization, it is hard to imagine that most decisions will be made to audiences unfamiliar to the decision maker. Still the decision maker needs to stay informed about their thinking, problems, and moods. Knowing the audience involves two concepts — prospecting and qualifying.

Prospecting for Support

Prospecting for support is the identification of individuals who appear on the surface to want or need your program or solution. If you select the audience, you prospect to determine who should be invited to be a member of the audience. If you face or will face an audience selected by someone else, you prospect the audience. Audience prospecting is identification of individuals in the audience who on the surface appear to have a need for the program or solution and will express the need earlier than other individuals in the audience.

Indicators of possible needs are called *leads*. Don't stifle your imagination about possible leads; there are many leads. The following are examples of leads which could be used for a board-room business audience.

1. Those who mentioned or complained about "the problem"
2. Those who owe favors
3. People seeking support of their programs

---

1. Richard P. Coleman, "The Significance of Social Stratification in Selling," in Martin L. Bell (ed.) *Marketing: A Maturing Discipline* (Chicago: American Marketing Association, 1961), pp. 171–84.
2. See Raymond A. Bauer, "The Role of the Audience in the Communication Process," summary in Stephen Greyser (ed.) *Toward Scientific Marketing* (Chicago: American Marketing Association, 1964), pp. 73–82.

4. Social contacts
5. Reference leads

The leads may make it possible to approach individuals before the meeting to find out whether they will give support and under what conditions that support is available. Leads can also be used within the meeting to alter the presentation, if the lead proves out.

Qualifying Prospects for Support

Prospecting was accomplished by surface identification of need. The qualifying step consists of the additional care taken to establish and assess the reality of the need, the authority necessary to obtain support, the willingness of the prospect to pay the price, and willingness to pay the price. An example of qualifying assessment in action begins with the question: Does the need exist? Does the particular person identified have a program or decision he or she wants support for? If the answer is no, the person is disqualified. If yes, next question: Does the person have the necessary authority within the group to lend the support desired?[3] Whose acceptance or which individual speaking out in favor would be most impressive? Even in committee decisions there is normally a key individual. It is not necessary, of course, that the most respected person speak out favorably, as long as someone with authority does speak and the most authority-carrying person is positive or remains neutral. The person who does not carry the authority (or worse is not respected) should be ignored. If the person has authority, will she or he be willing to support the program? The person may see the decision or program as a poor one or one with more potential for trouble than it is worth. In this case, the target has disqualified himself.

If the person is willing to give support, you must assess whether the strings attached are worth that person's support. Before abandoning a program, there may be additional qualifying steps for you to take — suggestions, alterations, and negotiation should be considered and attempted. Possibly better programs or decisions will result.

The One-Person Audience

Prospecting and qualifying a one-person audience selected by someone else would seem rather difficult; it does require variation. The one-person audience allows much more time to research an individual than would be possible with large audiences, an advantage which should produce better results. To vary the prospecting and qualifying process for the one-person audience, thinking should be in terms of ideas rather than people. You must identify ideas with which the person will agree. These ideas should, at least on the surface, be important ones related to the decision or program. Qualifying the ideas can take place in casual meetings before or during the presentation. Qualification in casual meetings before a presentation provides the opportunity for structuring the presentation around the qualified ideas.

---

3. Elihu Katz and Paul F. Lazarsfeld, *Personal Influence* (New York: Free Press of Glencoe, 1955).

Challenging Individuals in the Audience

Prospecting and qualifying should be a continuous process. It should occur throughout the presentation. Mistakes and the demand for more detail make continuous prospecting and qualifying necessary. Many types of individuals will be identified: some very much in agreement, some interested but hesitant, others with questions, comments and suggestions — all very pleasant and asking only for a small amount of your time and attention. Still there are a number of even more challenging types, for instance, "the chatterer."

The Chatterer

The chatterer wants to do all the talking. Possibilities for winning the support of the "chatterer" include giving her or him a chance to talk for a few minutes. Listening is an important part of presentation. After the chatterer has had some time to talk, interrupt and make comments about what has been said, working that person's ideas into a continuation of the presentation. If the chatterer starts to talk again, ask others to comment on his or her remarks. If their comments lend weight to what the chatterer was expressing, change the presentation to cover those areas. More likely, however, the comments will be neutral or negative toward the chatterer's ideas, whereupon, hopefully, the audience will settle down to make only pertinent comments. Avoid giving the chatterer too much of an opportunity to speak by avoiding looking directly at him. If the chatterer continues, tactfully suggest that someone else should have a chance or ask to see him or her after the meeting for comments or suggestions.

The Pot Shotter

A relative of the "chatterer," the "pot shotter," constantly tries to start an argument to catch you up. As with the chatterer, first listen before taking any action. It may be that the person is not really an arguer but has one area of genuine confusion and is seeking clarification. Does the person seem sincere in wanting to know? Usually it doesn't take too long to recognize a pot shotter because of a lack of sincerity about the points these people raise. Remember, the pot shotter has an objective: rattling, confusing, frustrating and getting a heated reaction from the speaker; therefore, avoid this temptation. Avoid becoming personal and insulting and never attempt to win an argument with such a person. You may be right, but you never *win*. Ask for verification and evidence— in other words, make him back his statements with facts. Another strategy is to refer the pot shotter's questions to the group and then back to her or him. With care, even the "pot shotter" can be won over and will give support.

Mr. and Ms. Meek

An entirely different type of problem is "Mr. or Ms. Meek." The meek may have good suggestions or comments and may want to support you, but may, for some reason, be unable to vocalize their thoughts. It is not to be assumed, of course, that the silent are in agreement with the program or decision. Only when their thoughts are brought out into the open, however, is it possible to deal with them. Recognition of the meek is a good approach for bringing them out. Call the person by name and ask for an opinion on a noncontroversial issue or an easy question. The risk of answering an easy question incorrectly is low. Once the conversation becomes easier, the more difficult questions may be asked. Meek persons often carry substantial weight when speaking out. Since they speak out seldom, people tend to listen.

Disinterested Partial Observer
Perhaps the most difficult types of all are the "disinterested partial observers."[4] As do the other types, they come in all shapes and forms: the sleepy heads, whispering visitors, readers, and so forth. Obviously, these people have to be pulled into the presentation. Try to make comments about how the program or decision will affect them. Ask direct questions of them about their area, about their thoughts, and point out how they may have already been affected or have taken steps in the direction you suggest. Work to get them involved.

As you make more and more presentations, you will see other types not mentioned here and discover even more effective ways of winning their support.

Lacing the Audience
Occasionally the need to lace the audience with preselected favorable individuals may arise. Most of the audience may be self-selecting or selected by someone else, but almost always the speaker has an opportunity to include some individuals with favorable or predetermined behavior. The trial attorney brings forth experts, witnesses, and the like; the auctioneer often has a person or two who will start the bid if it fails to start in a specified time; a politician may have someone in the audience to ask prepared questions; the comedian may have a stooge in the audience. These are all examples of lacing the audience. There are many reasons for lacing an audience: lack of confidence, generation of interest, speeding the presentation, and so forth. Lacing is a strategy worth some thought. It can work beautifully, but it can also be abused and, in some cases, may be unethical. The user always runs the risk that this strategy will have a detrimental effect — if, for example, the lawyer's expert lacks enough expertise.

Summary
You may feel, after reading the preceding sections on the audience, that such strategies are too political, unethical, or simply unnecessary. To the first criticism, the answer is "Yes, it is political," if political means considering your audience, its reaction, and enlisting some in

---

4. As a possible explanation for disinterest, see David O. Sears and Jonathan L. Freedman, "Selective Exposure to Information: A Critical Review," *Public Opinion Quarterly,* (Summer, 1967), pp. 194–213.

the audience to help win support of others. The difference between a decision maker who seems apolitical and the situation described in the preceding pages is that the seemingly apolitical decision maker is more subtle, astute, and capable of carrying through the procedure with little observable effort.

If trickery and deceit are involved, the application of the process is "unethical." Some people are unethical and abuse these strategies. How, though, can application of the process which considers other people — their wants, needs, opinions, and the like — in a positive way be considered unethical?

The audience must be considered in any presentation, because decision making, acceptance and implementation depend on people. Most programs and decisions require working with personalities who must be persuaded. Moreover, most problems have several answers and the "right" answer is not always obvious. Searching out early supporters becomes necessary when an atmosphere of hesitancy exists, an atmosphere characterized by differing philosophies, recent setbacks, and, general hesitancy about a little additional risk. The early vocal supporter can establish a more relaxed atmosphere, congenial to discussion of the decision.

The general philosophy behind Know Your Audience is to consider the audience and fashion decisions and programs to be acceptable to them. Giving the audience everything it wants is not desirable, nor is forcing unwanted decisions and programs upon them. Rather, the philosophy aims for a more cooperative and flexible atmosphere.

Know the Situation

Too often the presentation situation is treated the same from presentation to presentation. This treatment belies the fact that the situation can vary tremendously. A formal situation is obviously different from an informal situation. Both demand different consideration. Moreover, the amount of input you have in structuring the situation will vary. The discussions which follow assume considerable input.

Arranging the Time and Place

In arranging a time and place for the presentation, the ideal interview situation should be kept in mind. It should be uninterrupted, relaxed, informal, and conversational. All individuals have to be considered; a time and place convenient for everyone is most desirable. The person making the presentation will want sufficient time to prepare without delaying the presentation too far into the future. The people who will hear the presentation will want a time which fits into their schedules without stress.

The place should, of course, have the physical facilities to accommodate the presentation as prepared — screens, easels, chalkboards, and the like. The physical facilities should also allow for an uninterrupted presentation while accommodating those present in relative comfort. Often the physical aspects are given too little attention beforehand, and at the last minute, "complications" set in. Although the spur-of-the-moment informal meeting in the hallway can be effective in obtaining decisions or program support, complications can be a detriment to such meetings. Interruptions, wandering attention, lack of visual aids, and such, make the spur-of-the-moment informal meeting unreliable for more important programs and decisions, except as places to obtain tentative reactions.

Practical efforts should be made to choose the best possible time and place within the given constraints.

Obtaining Appointments

Although the straightforward approach — "I'd like to see you" — is an excellent approach for obtaining appointments when the person to be contacted is an acquaintance, there are other approaches. When scheduling a time with people you are less familiar with, or for variation with acquaintances, you may wish to contact the person socially to congratulate him or her, to discuss a letter mailed on some other action, or to "break the ice" by some similar pretext. There are multiple reasons for meetings or for contacting a person. Secondary reasons can be used successfully when they are intended and are interpreted as genuine interest in the person.

The appointment procedure should include introductions and other qualifying information that may be necessary. Capture the person's interest as quickly as possible, stress the benefits of the proposed meeting (time and place), and secure agreement about those important issues.

Approach at Meeting

Perhaps even more important than the presentation is the establishment of the atmosphere in the initial few minutes of the meeting.[5] The atmosphere established in the first minute may very well be the atmosphere which carries through the entire meeting. One important element of the atmosphere is conveying the feeling that you are in control. Control is interpreted as knowing what is occurring, why it is occurring, and what most of the problems and advantages are. This atmosphere should come from an air of confidence (not arrogance), aggressiveness, and initiative. To convey this impression requires planning. Appearance and manner have to be appropriate. In appearance, the styles and taste of the people at the meeting should be the guide. Your appearance does not have to be exactly the same; in fact, establishing yourself as an individual who is different, who thinks for her or himself is a good idea. Being radically different usually hampers rather than helps, however. The manners which almost always seem appropriate to convey are: enthusiasm, sincerity, courtesy, and consistency. Can enthusiam be faked? One theory

---

5. See Edward T. Hall, *The Silent Language* (New York: Fawcett Publications, Inc., 1961).

holds that by acting enthusiastic, eventually one becomes enthusiastic. Mental attitude does have much bearing on enthusiasm, as it does on sincerity, courtesy, and consistency. Manner through enthusiasm, sincerity, courtesy, and consistency also results from having and using, initially and throughout the meeting, personal information (names, ages, education, idiosyncrasies, hobbies, family) about the people in attendance.

A correct introduction can do much to establish a positive atmosphere. The correct introduction is one which makes people feel the time to be spent in the meeting is well worth it. Introductions are as important to friends as they are to complete strangers. You should first sell yourself and then your decisions or program.

Know Yourself

If we know anything, we know ourselves — at least we think we do. The problem is that we quite often fail to look at ourselves in the context of a specific situation. What are your strengths, weaknesses, and misconceptions in the presentation context?

Few people are really good at every phase of making presentations. Some individuals are good at making the formal part of presentations, others at answering questions and moderating. Others are good at explaining charts, graphs, and artwork, while others are good at actually making the graphs, charts, and artwork. Still others are good in front of a group, but only for a short time, while others have a good sense of balance for speaking and listening. The natural procedure to take in assessing strengths and weaknesses is to think of the ideal presentation. Based on the ideal presentation, a person should use past experience of making presentations or participating in similar activities to determine strengths and weaknesses. If experience is insufficient as an indicator, prepare and rehearse the ideal presentation; have unbiased observers analyze critically the entire presentation.

Once weaknesses are known they can be handled in two ways. If time permits, proficiency in the area can be obtained through effort and practice. When time is a limitation, someone else with offsetting strengths can be consulted to coach you or to actually make part of the presentation.

Know Your Presentation

The best way to win support of a program or decision is have a good program and present it well. There are numerous ways you can take the audience on an imaginary tour of your program. The tour should be well planned to contain a logical sequence of events; it should maintain interest, yet get across the facts by alternating emotion and fact; and it should efficiently utilize time. Throughout the planning of the

tour, anticipate questions, areas for thought, and points to be emphasized. Two common question areas are costs and timing. How much
is it going to cost? Why does it cost so much? Is it too early for such a
program? Failing to anticipate questions and trouble spots leads to
objections and rejection. Failing to emphasize interest points is opportunity lost.

The Presentation Plan
Other plans for analyzing problems and presenting solutions were suggested in an early chapter. As suggested then, each problem may be
analyzed and solved in a variety of ways. Still another plan for analyzing
and presenting is suggested in the following list. Ultimately the particular plan used is not as important as the results obtained. As long
as the plan produces results efficiently, fine!

1. Describe, define, and locate the problem, the need, or the opportunity.
2. *Describe all details* of the proposed solution.
3. *Show* the *competitive situation:* Why is this the best solution? What
   makes it different?
4. Present a current survey of the solution's feasibility—why and how it
   can be implemented (brief overview).
5. Display appraisals (opinions), financial data, and other support data.
6. Offer documented operating and cost *pro forma* statements: *substantiate every figure.*
7. Summarize—*Ask* for agreement, approval. Make the request.

Using the above plan of presentation or any other plan, you should
strive to:

1. Get the audience into the act—emotionally, if not physically.
2. Select words which paint desired images.
3. Dramatize by presenting hope, emotion, glamour—by appealing to
   any or all of the five senses.
4. Back up the drama with facts.
5. Obtain accuracy by checking and double-checking all of the facts.
6. Secure understanding by breaking the presentation into more readily
   understood parts, presenting a point, and backing it up with explanation and demonstration.
7. Secure understanding or assess the degree of comprehension by
   checking and rechecking through questions and careful listening.
8. Make the decision for approval easy.

Most people are unable to concentrate on a particular topic for very
long. Variation and change of pace helps to lengthen the span of attention. If, however, the presentation has to be long to cover all the facts,
take a break at a natural breaking point.

Finally, support data is accepted in direct relationship to the professional standing (in the profession and outside of it) of those who give it.
The janitor may know investments, but few people will accept his recommendations. In today's atmosphere, questioning the action and wisdom

of those with professional standing is not unheard of and should be expected.

Presentation Aids
The "straight" delivery can be effective when a presentation is extremely short or concerns a topic of extreme interest. Variations and aids of a number of types do often improve the presentation. These variations range from simple voice inflections to complicated audio-visual systems. In order to have such aids readily at your disposal, make a practice of noting and recording mentally—better yet recording on paper and fil-ing—good aids which you encounter. A particularly good joke at the right time can do much to enliven a session, and—more important—increase the effectiveness of a presentation, as can a quotation (even if you have to attribute it to your grandmother), a unique technique for involving the audience, a sample, a model, testimonials, charts and graphs, color renderings, and the like. Therefore, be a collector of presentation aids. It is essential that the collection be detailed—what

Exhibit 2   *Demonstration aids*

Photographs	Flip charts	Models
Sound filmstrips	Flash cards	Video tapes
Movies	Maps	Audio tapes
Overhead projectors	Scrapbooks	Telephone calls
Visuals	Exhibits or displays	Testimonials
Slides	Mock-ups	Expert witness
Presentation books	Blackboards	Pencil and paper
Portfolios	Graphs	
Charts	Flannel boards	

was the joke, how was it worked into the presentation, with what kind of subject would it be compatible, on what did its success as an aid depend? For example, an analogy used often and effectively in talks on politics, economy, and philosophy was the story of a father busily trying to meet a deadline on an important task while being constantly badgered by his young son to play. The father noticed a map (nation, country, or state—whatever the presentation covered); he took the map and tore it into many small pieces, telling his son to put it back together again, thinking it would take a long time because of the many lines. In a very short time, the son was back with the map completely together. When his father asked how he reassembled it so quickly, the child said, "It was easy: there was a picture of a man on the other side and once you have the man together you have the world together." Collecting is one thing; having the aids at your finger tips at the right time is another. Unless you have a good memory, a system helps. For quota-tions, jokes, and the like, there are many books with such compilations. Their organization as well as subject matter can be used.

Much finger-tip readiness stems from organization. Some, however, also stems from inventorying the aids. For audio-visual equipment, one should know what the organization has in the way of equipment, what the equipment's capabilities are, and when and where it can be used. Knowing the amount of lead time necessary is very important, also. Last-minute ordeals of setting up and trying to use complicated equipment are hectic and unnecessarily distracting. For obtaining equipment from outside the organization, a shortened lead time may mean a substantial increase in cost. The cost of aids should be a known factor — many are quite expensive and their use should be optimized by spreading them over multiple applications.

In summary, effort should be expended toward using presentation aids by:

1. Being a collector
2. Organizing
3. Having an inventory knowledge of available equipment
4. Being aware of lead times and other conditions
5. Knowing costs and trying to find multiple uses to lower cost per use

Slide Films and Sound Tract
As an example of one presentation aid and its advantages when used correctly, consider slides with the inaudible beeper sound tract. When set up, the slide projector is keyed to advance a slide at the signal of an inaudible beep on the sound tract. Clearly, such a system has many advantages as an aid. If the room is not totally darkened, it presents a good opportunity for total concentration on feedback from the audience through observation or other use of the time free from direct presenting. Because the sound tract must be produced before the presentation, a carefully written script can be used and the tract can be recorded and rerecorded until just the right timing and voice inflection are obtained. The sound quality and the pictures also produce an effect. Slides, of course, can be produced by *anyone* with a 35mm camera and a closeup attachment, but the overall appearance of such a presentation is one of professionalism. The system also has flexibility: the slides can be used without the sound tract and rearranged without difficulty. Such a system is quite portable, too. The most outstanding feature, however, is the power with which the message is impressed upon the mind of the audience.

Criteria for Using Presentation Aids
An aid should meet certain criteria before it is employed in a presentation. First, it should help advance the objective and purpose of the presentation — to win support. If the aid detracts because it is sloppy, unprofessional, or too professional (too slick), it is not serving its function. Aids should encourage attention to the objective, not divert it. Well-utilized aids should:

1. Help change the pace of the presentation delivery.
2. Illustrate differences and similarities to develop understanding, providing contrast.
3. Generate interest.
4. Provide the unexpected to maintain attention.

Good use of aids demand good timing, much planning, and a lot of effort. First impressions, after seeing the successful application of presentation aids, may lead to use of a number of elaborate aids. Situational demands, however, normally lead to the use of aids which are more simple in nature. If you plan to use such aids, expect to put some work into them.

Overcoming Nervousness

A natural condition before a presentation is a feeling of nervousness. Even the best performers admit to feeling "butterflies." Nervousness is a desirable condition in moderate doses. A moderate amount stimulates a person, encouraging a good performance. Extreme nervousness, however, can lead to avoidance or cancellation of the presentation. It can also lead to silly mistakes and awkwardness.

The problem then is to reduce extreme nervousness and control it generally. The best solution to nervousness is a well-prepared presentation. If you *know what you are talking about* and know you know what you are talking about, 95 percent of the problem is solved. Sometimes, good preparation still leaves a feeling of nervousness. The most obvious next step is to do a dry run — after appropriate rehearsals — of the entire presentation in front of a small (perhaps only one-person) audience who will critique with gusto. If possible, the audience should be made up of two individuals: one with expertise in presentation skills and the other with expertise in the subject matter. Rework the presentation with their suggestions in mind.

Before and during the presentation, a relaxing technique can be employed. There are limitations on what these activities can be. Before the presentation, more possible techniques are appropriate than during the presentation. During the presentation, the technique should not be visible to the audience or, at least, not distracting. Several deep breaths or a breathing exercise could be used before the presentation, for example. During the presentation, the activity might have to be limited to something mental — for example, perceiving oneself in the most friendly atmosphere conceivable with members of the audience could be a useful mental relaxing activity.

Success, of course, can work wonders in reducing hesitancy and nervousness in future presentations. Unfortunately, sometimes we fail.

Tried and Failed

After having painstakingly arrived at a decision or having devised a program and gone to extraordinary effort to present it, we may find that it fails to win support. Let's consider for a moment how to fail successfully. Failing is a subject few like to look at in personal terms. One reason for refusing to recognize the possibility of failure is the tremendous concentration on success required in a difficult situation to produce the needed confidence and effort. Doubt — the possibility of failure — generates nervousness and curbs effectiveness. It may lead to a lack of desire even to try. But the possibility of failure encourages the success-seeker to plan, to anticipate, to take care of details, and to seek out information.

Any presentation of a decision or program involves approval both of the decision or program and of the program designers and supporters. The two go together. Complete separation is impossible, although in the throes of failure we want to assign the fault to the program, not ourselves. Complete separation is impossible, however, since any program or decision which requires input of time and effort on the part of the individual also requires psychological investment — failure hurts. Unfortunately, there are individuals who have been unable to cope with success and, though great planners, organizers and so forth, they manage somehow to insure failure by self-defeating behavior.

Assuming success is really the desired objective, when failure seems imminent, the first question should be, "Will the program still work?" Failure can sometimes be more perceived than actual and it need not be total. Therefore, one should try to improve the program, the presentation, the timing, and reestablish the need for the program before giving up. The changes may make the decision or program a smashing success, even though the original program failed initially. Salvaging a program is a part of succeeding at failure. Quite often, when support is not immediately apparent, a program is perceived as failure when it should be perceived as merely requiring further proof that support is deserved. Persistency is a necessary element in pulling success out of failure.

Sometimes salvage of a program is possible, but there are times when we must admit that the program as a whole was insufficient. To admit to a mistake, to give up on a program, is a difficult task, but occasionally an unavoidable one. When we have to admit failure of a program, efforts should then be aimed at salvage of the person. As already stated, a personal investment is involved in every decision or program into which a person puts time and effort. When a program fails, the perceived psychological loss may be much greater than external investment would imply. To reduce this possibility, we should ask ourselves what psychological returns were received, even from failure, that will help ensure the success of future decisions and programs. What did we learn? Almost always something to promote future success will be salvaged. A personal accounting is also helpful. After listing strengths and assets, an individual will find that the losses from any one decision or program gone bad are quite small. Resilience is a necessary and desirable quality, which we should develop and help others to develop. If you have become more resilient because of failure, you have failed successfully.